THE ALTAR GUILD BOOK

by

Barbara Gent

and

Betty Sturges

Morehouse-Barlow, Co., Inc.
Wilton, Connecticut

Copyright© 1982 Barbara Gent and Betty Sturges

Morehouse-Barlow Co., Inc.
78 Danbury Road
Wilton, Connecticut 06897

ISBN 0-8192-1305-5

Library of Congress Catalog Card Number 82-80469

Printed in the United States of America

Table of Contents

Foreword

I live near sand dunes. While I am no student of them I am observant enough to know that many of them walk—constantly moving and changing shape. While their outward appearance is regularly altering, the basic form or concept called "dune" is always there.

It seems to me that the same is true of our worship of God. The need for and the basic elements of worship are constant, but the expression and the means we use are constantly changing. Our Prayer Book is a prime example. Certainly the basic elements of worship are brought together in it. Then both old and new means of expression and response are provided to enable us to worship and to live it. Change need not destroy, for change can enliven and illumine.

It is because of this that I am delighted to commend *The Altar Guild Book*. The authors have been regular and creative in worship and have served the Body of Christ through Parish, Diocesan, and in Betty's case, National Altar Guilds. Long ago they both discovered that change does not automatically or necessarily destroy. Holding to the basic ideas and principles of worship, they have embraced the 1979 Prayer Book and have found it to reveal and illustrate those basic principles.

The tone of this book frees us to be creative and imaginative in the local Parish Altar Guild. Filled with much historical and technical material this manual is a clear encouragement for the local priest and altar guild to develop their own guidelines for worship. But always there is the quiet reminder that we are the people of a book who need to discover anew what it means to live freely within the guidelines and rubrics of that Book. Needs and opportunities vary. All parishes do not have the same traditions or resources or current opportunities, just as a standard across-the-board altar guild book of rules and actions no longer seems to fit our needs. The authors do a good job in allaying fears that still persist about doing things our own way to speak to our own situation. Written as it is, I feel it will be helpful to all traditions within our church.

I find this a creative book and one that supplies a rationale for imaginative creativity. It has been my privilege to know and to have worked closely with each of these women and the respect I have grown to have for them is the respect I have for their book.

The Right Reverend Morgan Porteus
Bishop of Connecticut, Retired

Preface

Our stint in the altar guild ministry in the last forty years has been a double journey. We have both traveled the path from the strict training in altar guild procedures of the forties through the confusions of that training in the fifties and sixties by variations in ceremonial and by the trial services. Now we have come to the 1979 *Book of Common Prayer* when training in particulars no longer seems practical for altar guilds because such training doesn't apply universally.

Besides this journey which was extremely unsettling at times, we have throughout the same forty years had a second experience. We both have had the privilege of worshiping in Episcopal churches throughout this country. Our own lives have taken us into churches north, south, east and west, and beyond-the-parish altar guild responsibilities. Our worship away from home has been a boon because altar guild background, like background in any other discipline, sharpens the eye and the ear to the familiar, and we have grown in our understanding of liturgy because of it.

As a result, we have for a long time known about the variety in liturgical practice existing in our Church even under the 1928 Prayer Book and about the adjustments many altar guilds had obviously made in "standard manual procedure" in order to do what they were doing. With the advent of the 1979 *Book of Common Prayer*, variety in ceremonial has become the norm for the Episcopal Church and church people everywhere are awakening to differences in liturgical practice. The spirit of freedom in celebrating the new liturgy has brought us face to face wherever we have been with questions from altar guild members confused and challenged by that freedom. These people want to know the "right way." The overall answer to these questions is: "There are many ways; the right way for you is the way your priest prefers." This fresh approach to the altar guild ministry requires greater knowledge about liturgy than has been common to altar guilds and acquaintance with the many possibilities open to those who prepare places for worship.

This book is the result. We have attempted to include in one binding enough information to answer the common questions we are asked about altar guild background, both general and specific, and to provide some guidelines for carrying out altar guild assignments where they seem appropriate. Throughout the book we emphasize that there isn't a standard way, a "correct" way, to conduct the liturgy of the Episcopal Church. Beyond a few rubrics in *The Book of Common Prayer* which bind us to certain words and certain actions, we are free in our communities to work out our own ways for carrying out our worship under the guidance of our priests. Ultimately the priest with whom the guild works is its tutor; its ministry is an extension of that priest's liturgical responsibility to the parish community.[1]

We are both grateful to the priests who first called us into this ministry and to those who have guided and supported us along the way. We thank the many other priests whose words, spoken and written, have nurtured our thinking about liturgy during these years, and all the altar guild women and men who have worked with us and taught us, lessons large and small, especially Mary Chester Buchan and Elizabeth Randall-Mills, whose direction was part of our beginnings. We owe a great dept to W. Christian Koch and Byron D. Stuhlman, priests and chairmen of the Liturgical Commissions of the Dioceses of Massachusetts and Connecticut respectively, and to Morgan Porteus, retired Bishop of Connecticut, for their wise and thoughtful suggestions after reading our manuscript. As for our husbands, we acknowledge that this time of writing has pushed them aside more than once. To them, for their cooperative forbearance and understanding, our love.

Barbara Gent
Betty Sturges

The Altar Guild Book

The Altar Guild Book is designed to provide background material for altar guild members old and new and for anyone else assigned to prepare church buildings and altars for worship. It is an information book, not a manual. Manuals indicate "standard procedure," and the liturgical study of the mid-twentieth century has shown that the "standard procedure" presented and kept alive in altar guild manuals is largely custom, at times adhered to and at other times not. Through the years most ceremonial has depended on local circumstances and has been changeable. There have been many types of buildings in which to worship, many kinds of vessels, vestments, linens, and other church furnishings to use in worship, and many ways to prepare them for that use. All have been acceptable in their time and place and all have gone through change.

Worship, as Christians understand it, is an offering of their life in thanksgiving to God for his gift of that life redeemed. Christians aren't uniform. When they gather to worship as members of the Body of Christ, they are individuals acting in concert to celebrate the freedom he has given them. "Standard procedure" with its "shoulds" and "musts," its concerns about "proper" and "correct," runs counter to this sense of freedom. It restricts the joy of Pentecost and prevents worshipers offering their own gifts in worship.

The Book of Common Prayer (1979) teaches that, within the general guidelines set by the rubrics, worship can vary. Preparation for worship can also vary. It can vary as widely as the talents, imaginations, resources and circumstances of each worshiping community. Uniformity is in the central act of each sacrament, not in the manner of its performance. The Prayer Book assures certain uniformities by binding rubrics, but it introduces variety in performance by wording other rubrics permissively or by omitting rubrics entirely. In effect, each worshiping group is freed to express its own life in most of its ceremonial not only from parish to parish, but within each parish as well, from week to week, season to season and year to year.

As a result, the manuals familiar to altar guilds, even with updating and local editing, no longer provide enough material to guide all altar preparers everywhere through the intricacies of making the church ready for all services of worship. There are countless ways, and the Prayer Book invites all worshiping communities to find their own.

With their new freedom, altar guild workers have an increased responsibility and so do priests. Those who prepare places for worship need more background than they did when they could depend on fixed printed rules to guide them. In order to do what they are now called to do, it is important for them to be taught at least something of the theology of the sacraments and other worship services. They need to become thoroughly familiar with their own situations—with their priests' ideas, their fellow parishioners' feelings and attitudes, and their own resources of time, talent and money. They also need to stay abreast of the constant changes in art, technology, society and the economy in respect to the ways all four affect altar equipment and church traditions. They have to find answers to new questions that stem from new ideas, new products and new challenges in all these areas.

People who prepare church buildings for worship really need parochial manuals which incorporate everything that they will find helpful in doing their work, loose-leaf (or card file) manuals which can be revised and updated easily and regularly as conditions (or priests) change. In order to produce manuals which cover both the general philosophy of altar guild ministry and the particulars for carrying out that ministry locally, altar guilds need supervision and support from their priests and information about what is happening in the Church today, both liturgically and practically. They gather this kind of information from their priests, experience, observation and books.

The Altar Guild Book is a book to start with. It looks at the altar guild ministry as a whole. It looks at its background, its purpose, its varied structure. The book contains material about vestments and vessels, linens and hangings, flowers and candles, housekeeping and preparation for worship, relating to both yesterday and today. Throughout the text page references are included to rubics in the 1979 *Book of Common Prayer* that affect altar guild work. The bibliography provides a list of books for further reading. *The Altar Guild Book* is intended to help parishes create their own manuals.

Forty-some years ago John Baillie wrote a prayer[2] which speaks clearly to altar guilds today:

Give me an open mind, O God, a mind ready to receive and to welcome such new light of knowledge as it is Thy will to reveal to me. Let not the past ever be so dear to me as to set a limit to the future. Give me courage to change my mind, when that is needed. Let me be tolerant to the thoughts of others and hospitable to such light as may come to me through them. Amen.

Yesterday and Today

Origins

Altar guilds as the Episcopal Church has known them developed in the late nineteenth century, a natural outgrowth of what had been from the beginning an exclusively male world. In the early days of the Church, when followers of Christ gathered in private homes to break bread together and share their memories of him, presumably the head of the household provided whatever was required for the meal. As Christians multiplied and needed larger buildings in which to meet, certain people were given the ministry of caring for these places, and the worshipers themselves provided the food for the meal (and for their leaders and the poor besides). By the fourth century, the parochial ministry as known today had been generally established, and for hundreds of years thereafter the lesser clergy (later called sacristans) were responsible for everything that is now considered "altar guild work." A sacristan supervised the sacristy and all the paraphernalia of worship, prepared for services and did the church housekeeping as well.

In the early Church of England altar care was also the task of lesser priests such as the sacristan and verger in the cathedral and the clerk (cleric) in the parish. Years later laymen became the sacristans and eventually women were included in this ministry. Percy Dearmer's words about the duties of the sacristan "who had much better be a layman," written about 1900, tell the altar guild story for both England and the United States at that time.[3]

> The sacristan's position is a most important one, and he must be devout, sensible, and even-tempered . . . He need not do a very great deal himself, but he must see that everything is done, which means that he must be kind and pleasant in manner as well as careful. He should have a general knowledge of the matters he has to deal with . . . He will see that a list of servers is posted on the wall for every service in the week . . . He will see

1

that everything is ready five minutes before service begins on Sunday—the vestments laid out, the candles lit by a taperer, and the charcoal heated by the thurifer. He will gently superintend the band of helpers who are needed if everything is to be kept as the things pertaining to God's worship ought to be kept. For many duties women are best, only they need to have their realms well-defined and protected, and unless they are responsible to the sacristan there may sometimes be trouble . . . A lady will often be needed to put out the (servers') vestments every day, and her work will require much neatness of method. She may also be responsible for washing and mending the albes [sic], etc., of clergy and servers. Another may be needed to polish the brass work and to trim the candles . . . (a lad may clean the brass and other metal, but women are more reliable, and men cannot generally spare sufficient time). Another may be needed to dust the high altar and see to the altar-cloths, and another to see to the chapel. Often another lady . . . can undertake the useful task of washing the purificators . . . If there are several helpers, each responsible for his or her own piece of work, and all responsible to the Sacristan, and through him to the Parson, the most perfect cleanliness and order can be secured . . .

Sometime in the nineteenth century, women became assistants to sacristans, at least in the Anglican part of the Church. By the turn of the twentieth century they were beginning to organize into "altar guilds," and in most places in the United States they assumed the sacristan's duties themselves under the guidance of their priests. Throughout this century women have predominated in altar guild membership. Until the 1970s this channel was the only one through which they could serve God at the altar. Occasionally, however, men have proved to be as helpful to women in altar guilds as women once were to the men in Percy Dearmer's sacristy, and now in the 1980s men are taking part in increasing numbers. They serve as sacristans, designers, craftsmen, flower arrangers, embroiderers, candle makers and just plain caretakers of the house of the Lord. Once again the decoration of the church and preparation for worship is becoming a joint lay ministry.

In several churches today this joint lay ministry extends beyond the bounds of a formal altar guild organization, and preparation for worship has become the responsibility of the parish family. Small groups from the worshiping community (family units, for example, parents and children together) carry out all the tasks traditionally done by altar guilds before a service. They work on a regular basis, perhaps twelve groups, each for a month at a time, cleaning, readying the worship centers and things of worship, even supplying the bread and wine. In some instances, special groups are responsible for special occasions (weddings, funerals, Christmas) and special tasks (laundry, flowers, repairs), but in others the basic group does everything.

This "parish family" method of altar care also appears in various kinds of institutions: summer camps, retirement homes, hospitals, prisons, conference centers, religious houses, and the like. In these places, members of the community (residents or staff) are often those charged with the care and preparation of the altar for services.

In all these circumstances involving people not formally organized and trained as altar guilds, guidelines for the specific situation worked out by the priest-in-charge are indispensible if the preparation for worship is to run smoothly and easily and be a joyful offering to the Lord. Although the term "altar guild" is used throughout this book because it is the familiar one for this special ministry in the Church, the material in the book is intended for any group engaged in caring for the altar and its furnishings.

Transition

The difficulty some altar guild members have in accepting changes in their procedure today comes from their almost too strict training yesterday, itself the result of change that altar guilds faced in another era. In the days of Percy Dearmer's women assistants to the sacristan, the women's work was primarily housekeeping, special housekeeping with some unusual tasks, but housekeeping nevertheless. Preparation for the rites and ceremonies of the Church was the sacristan's (and his male helpers') assignment. What he needed was help in keeping the church and its furnishings "decent and in order."

This situation had not changed appreciably when women first banded into altar guilds in the United States. Then, early in this century in some areas, much later in others, "seasonal colors" and historic Eucharistic vestments started to appear for the first time in the Episcopal Church.[4] In this same period the clergy in many parishes encouraged more frequent celebrations of the Holy Communion than the monthly or quarterly celebrations that were customary. They also began adding ceremonial historically attached to that rite by including lavabo, incense, bells and the like. Altar guilds found they had to learn many things in order to do whatever had to be done to prepare their churches for the new departures in worship.

At first they learned from their priests, later from little handbooks written especially for them, filled with precise details about each aspect of preparation. They learned terms, routines and historic customs as well as questionable taboos and allegories. They learned what was then known or believed about ceremonial tradition and their responsibilities expanded far beyond simple housekeeping. They learned to dress the altar, set the credence, prepare the chalice, lay out the vestments, make the linens and launder them in specific ways, arrange flowers and place and light candles, following directions presented as if there were only one way to perform these tasks. The teaching of priests was similar, but not identical. The various handbooks were also similar, but not identical. Although adaptation of instructions to local situations frequently proved convenient for teaching or necessary for performance and some-times spread to other parishes, altar guild training, all in all, was uniform. It bred women devoted to the altar guild ministry and produced altar guilds basically of one mind in understanding what was expected of them. Parishes may have differed in specific practices but altar guilds usually were not alert to these differences because the handbooks didn't acknowledge them. In fact, members became so conscientious about adhering exactly to what they had been taught that they assumed a "right way" that didn't exist and considered deviations from it "wrong." They found change of any kind unthinkable.

Change happens, though, in the Church as in the rest of life, and in the Church it is just as difficult to adjust to as elsewhere. Intense training for nearly a century in a single way to prepare a church build-ing for worship (the Eucharist or any other service) has compounded the problem for altar guilds. The uncertainties of that other time of changing rites and ceremonies are forgotten because the new customs of those years have so long been the status quo. The idea that worship practices have varied from age to age and place to place contradicts traditional altar guild thinking and experience, but it is a historical reality.

Now, in another time of the Church, that reality is at the heart of altar guild instruction. New liturgical insight has made many familiar old words and ceremonies redundant because ideas and practices that are far older in the Church have been incorporated in the worship services. New world conditions have introduced new situations in parishes, new problems to which old customs do not speak. New inventions have raised questions about the efficiency of old products, but new is neither right nor wrong, it is just new. In former ages the Church incorporated in its worship the new of its time, giving it place beside the old. Today the Church does the same. There is space for both Gothic and A-Frame, for an altar on the east wall and an altar in the nave, for brocade and polyester. Whether the bread and the wine are presented in silver or earthenware, the Lord Christ comes, and whether the people of God stand or kneel they receive him with thanksgiving.

Generally Speaking

Altar guilds today are groups of men and women organized in different ways who are called to serve God by preparing and tending the places where his people worship him. Their work is a thank-offering of time and many talents, a ministry of love undertaken in the name of Christ.

Altar work goes on quietly behind the scenes. What altar workers do is often unnoticed because average worshipers do not ordinarily think about the usual furnishings of altar and sanctuary. Worshipers often don't consider who has put out the furnishings and who cares for them. These two responsibilities, however, have been basic to altar guilds however organized. Some do very little else. Others may shoulder a wide range of responsibilities besides, like making or purchasing vestments and linens; managing flower monies and orders as well as arranging the flowers; replenishing (even making) the supply of bread, wine and candles; creating objects of art of various kinds for use or decoration; teaching church school classes, acolytes or other church groups about the things of worship; advising about memorial gifts for use in the sanctuary; participating in special rites like the stripping of the altar on Maundy Thursday. What altar guild workers are asked to do and how they are organized depends on the priest they work with and the place in which they work.

Unlike most other parish organizations, an altar guild or any other group of altar workers is not involved in parish business or social matters, but is the priest's partner in making the worship life of the parish run smoothly. Normally, selection of people to prepare the altar is a thoughtful process because of the closeness of their working relationship with the priest and the importance of their part in the parish liturgical life. Altar work is a vocation; workers are called to it and their response has to be a "Here am I" (Is. 6:8), for the work requires a willingness, as Bishop Lawrence said years ago, "to give more of their time and of themselves than is usually asked by the Church."[5] Talent and know-how are always useful attributes, but loyalty and commitment are essential if the priest is to lead the parish in worship with equanimity.

If a priest wants a traditional altar guild to care for equipment and prepare for services, that priest is the head of that guild but as a rule appoints a suitable person, man or woman, to superintend its work. (This person is sometimes called a directress or director, sometimes a coordinator, or a president.) The priest arranges for other officers or chairmen if the situation warrants, calls men and women to serve, and instructs them carefully (or provides for their instruction) in all aspects of preparation for all services of the Church.

A traditional altar guild is not the only answer to altar care and preparation in a parish and a priest may very well choose to follow some other practice. The priest may even decide to change in the midst of tenure from a well-functioning traditional altar guild to another system of altar care. If this situation arises in a parish, an established altar guild may need to be reminded that it exists only because the priest has asked it to and its ministry in the sanctuary is determined only by the priest's need for it.

The corollary of all this is that no group of people caring for the altar in a parish is meant to go on forever, much less an altar guild leader. All successive priests have the privilege of making their own appointments and arranging for the care of the altar and preparation for worship in their parishes. Bishop Lawrence, again: "It should be recognized by altar guild members that there is of necessity a variety of tradition, custom and practice within our Church; and the wishes of one rector may be very different from those of another. The present rector's orders are the 'orders of the day.' "[6] So although a new priest in a parish may find an "inherited directress/director" and an "inherited guild" adaptable and cooperative (or an inherited "other practice" working successfully), it is customary for all to resign (or to be ready to resign when convenient) to enable the new priest to select a new group or not to select one, if that seems preferable.

Altar guild organization has to be a local matter because each parish situation is different. Some altar guilds have only one worker, some as many as fifty. Some eventually involve the entire parish family. Some divide tasks according to expertise, some share them equally. Some prepare for worship in teams of two to five or more, some individually, and some assign duty for a month at a time, some for a week. Some meet frequently for planning, instruction and fellowship; some meet infrequently. Responsibilities vary widely from parish to parish, as do working conditions, time, talent and resources of workers. However convenient it might be to pretend that all altar guilds will fit into one organizational mold, it is unrealistic.

Organization of some kind is important just as it is for any other group that shares a continuing charge with exacting details. Some system has to be devised in each parish to ensure that preparation for every worship occasion will be completed on time according to the priest's wishes. Working such a system out and implementing it is a coordinator-priest responsibility. In so doing it is helpful for both to keep in mind that an altar guild "works together separately" and produces dependable results only when the separate units are given detailed directions. Each parish altar guild needs extensive guidelines for its own procedure, its own handbook or a locally annotated general manual. It needs a schedule tailored to its workers' available time, particularly if many of them are employed in business. It needs thoughtful assignment of special tasks with generous consideration of workers' enthusiasms and talents. It needs careful instruction for new participants, regular review for older participants, and constant updating for all to keep abreast of change. The group also needs opportunities for all workers to meet as a whole for a sense of the togetherness that gives them their reason for working separately as well as an understanding of their common task. Meeting regularly in "fellowship, in the breaking of bread and in the prayers" (p. 304) deepens the bond of shared ministry.

The bond among altar guild members extends beyond the parish through the ministry of larger altar guild organizations—diocesan, provincial and national. The primary purpose of all these is to support parish altar guilds by serving as resource centers for them. All three relay pertinent information; open up opportunities for learning about subjects related to altar work through conferences, meetings, publications and program materials; and encourage and facilitate the redistribution of used ecclesiastical furnishings. (For further information, see Appendix I.)

As changes in liturgy and in the world catapult parish altar guilds into successive tomorrows, the purpose of these larger groups becomes more and more meaningful. Invariably a question in one parish has been answered in another somewhere, and through the interchange of information parish to parish, diocese to diocese, across the country, it is possible for questions and answers to meet. Apart from all their other projects, the national, provincial and diocesan altar guilds serve parishes well through an efficient communications network.

The Work Room

A sacristy is a room in a church or parish house where vestments, hangings, linens, vessels and the other furnishings and housekeeping equipment used by altar guilds are kept. Most parish churches have a working sacristy, large or small, efficiently designed or makeshift. Some churches have a priest's sacristy (vestry, vesting room) as well. Some churches do not have adequate space for any real sacristy, so the altar guild workers prepare for the Eucharist and other services and care for altar equipment as well as they can without one. Many ingenious sacristies have been created by distraught altar guilds seeking a room of their own.

No two sacristies are alike, but all share the common characteristic of providing as efficient a center for church housekeeping as possible and having as many closets, drawers and shelves as space allows. To describe preferred types of drawers or closets is useful primarily to parishes designing new sacristies or redoing old ones. If storage places can be built to accommodate the shapes and sizes of the items to be stored, they become as useful as well-designed cupboards in a kitchen. Adjustable shelves, shallow drawers and divided closets are worth considering as is a really secure safe for valuable objects. Specific suggestions for storing linens, hangings and vestments are included in those chapters, and Appendix II is a description of a useful working sacristy.

If an altar guild looks at the tasks it is expected to do and the possessions it has to store, with a practiced homemaking eye, it will soon discern the best use of its available space. Each group has to work out its own plan. The most important precept for it to keep in mind is that no sacristy design is final. Even though it is a good idea for every item in current use to have a home of its own and for every storage space to be clearly labeled, no space belongs forever to the item stored in it. Storage space can be reassigned and revamped as equipment and parish needs change.

Preparing a Place

Altar guild workers prepare for all worship services including morning and evening prayer and the other offices as well as all the sacramental rites, but the Sunday Eucharist is the service that involves the greatest effort and the most knowledge. If the other services take place by themselves, they call for minimal preparation and very little equipment—a baptismal bowl, a funeral pall or wedding kneelers, flowers, candles, and a few vestments. The 1979 *Book of Common Prayer* is Eucharistically centered and the Eucharist is written so that it can encompass most of these other services as the Liturgy of the Word. If they are conducted in this way, preparation for them becomes part of the greater preparation for the Eucharist itself.

The Eucharist is not a last minute happening. Although it is "the principal act of Christian worship on the Lord's Day" (and increasingly on most other occasions when Christians gather to worship), the people of God are all preparing for it every day of their lives. In addition, some people make special preparations in order for it to happen each time. Whether a service is to be in the church building or away from it, bakers and winemakers, artisans and artists, vestry and sexton, choir and secretary, priest and altar guild, all have tasks to do well before the appointed hour. The altar guild prepares the place.

Preparing a place for the Eucharist is preparing for a family celebration. Cleaning house; decorating suitably for the guest of honor with flowers, candles and hangings; setting the table with the best linens and dishes; dressing up. All these are part of preparing for any celebration. For the Great Festival where Christ comes regularly to be with his followers in the Breaking of the Bread, each familiar act becomes especially significant. The whole task of getting ready to celebrate acquires overtones of holiness.

To make Eucharist, after the lessons and prayers are read, worshipers may gather around a plain wood table (or some other flat surface) with no covering except a clean white cloth and no ornaments. They may give the presider wine in a bottle with which to fill a cup of some kind large enough for the group (adding a little water), and a loaf of bread to place on some kind of serving dish. Then the Liturgy of the Table can begin. Relatively little preparation is needed for such a simple meal.

Altar guild workers build from that base in preparing any place for the Eucharist, as the Church from its beginning has built from that base. They bring in their symbols of joy and light and freedom and beauty to turn the simple meal into a feast of thanksgiving. The rubrics of the Eucharist require a table spread with a clean white cloth during the celebration, bread, wine, a little water and a cup. That's all. The other rubrics for the Eucharist which refer to church furnishings are suggestive, not binding, worded with "it is appropriate, it is desirable," and "may." Whatever else altar guild workers add to prepare for each occasion, they add under the direction of their priest, sometimes in collaboration with a parish liturgical committee. Options are as diverse as talent, imagination, resources and good taste allow.

In most cases, the place for worship is already "there" and an altar guild's addition and rearrangements have to be within that framework. Additions may be traditional or contemporary, old or new, practical or decorative, simple or ornate. If whatever is added becomes part of the whole and beautifies it, fits the occasion, adds to the service and doesn't disturb the worshiping group, it is suitable. The point is to intensify worship experience, not to distract the worshipers.

It is important for everyone concerned to know that things do not have to be formally dedicated to God to be suitable for use in a church. Improvised hangings, vessels, linens and vestments, auxiliary candle and flower holders, even substitute altars can enhance the liturgy. They become suitable when they are endowed with their new Church purpose by being put in place lovingly for a time.

The way altar guild workers perform their tasks is crucial to their ministry. Their dedication is to service in the name of the Lord, not to getting a job done. In "preparing the place" their concern is to create a setting for worship that is as whole, as complete, as they can possibly make it, using the resources and time and talents they have been given. Wholeness is related to holiness, to spiritual health, so their first step is to prepare themselves for ministry at the altar, to detach themselves from their own busy worlds for a time and offer their hands and their thoughts to God. Most altar workers begin their assignment in prayer. Then they proceed to cleaning and decorating. They are careful about housekeeping details, more so than they would ordinarily be. They are gentle with the things they touch, as if these were their own most precious treasures. They are considerate of each other's contributions, as they hope others will be of theirs. They are willing to give as much time as it takes to do what has to be done.

A gentle touch for the ornaments of worship is important, but there is a pitfall. At the outset of their service, altar guild workers learn to handle these objects carefully because of their value, real and sentimental. Often they are made of fine materials and were very expensive. Often they are one-time gifts and very old. Often they are difficult or impossible to repair or replace if damaged. So like all lovely things, they last longer if they are treated well. These objects also have been set aside for the liturgical life of the Church giving them special importance to the parish family. Because of this too altar guild workers handle them carefully. The objects play a special part in the family's worship life. For some reason, however, the idea of their being dedicated for use in the Church to give glory to God has sometimes become confused with godliness. The objects are often confused with their purpose and people think of them as "holy."

Objects can be touched by holiness but they are not holy themselves. When the people who handle them are dedicated to giving glory to God by serving in the Church with love at the core of their ministry, they fill the place they work in and surround the objects they handle with love and with holiness. Without the extra ingredient in the gentle touch, the valuable objects of the Church are just valuable objects.

So with the place that is being prepared for celebration. All the decorating is just decorating unless the Great Festival is the focus of the decorators. That mystery is the center of their work. "The whole task acquires overtones of holiness" from the way it is carried out. The place becomes a holy place again and again when love is in the preparation.

Cleaning the House

Cleaning is the first step in preparing a place for the Eucharist or any other service of worship. Cleaning not only includes the sanctuary and chancel, but the other worship areas of the church building and the sacristy as well. Even temporary worship places such as halls, informal outdoor chapels and sick rooms need to be neat and orderly before being used for worship. The goal of good church housekeeping is a sparkling house.

In general, altar guild workers sweep and dust, scrub and shine, trim and straighten, using their combined know-how to do their assigned tasks well. Some altar guilds have full care of the worship centers of the church, some are assisted by the sexton/verger, and occasionally by professional cleaning people. Some work in teams and share all housekeeping chores equitably each time they work. Others assign the housekeeping chores on a regular basis to specific persons, often by request, leaving only the sacristan duties to be shared before a service. Some altar guilds schedule special sessions for special work such as polishing silver, brass and wood; mending linens and vestments; cleaning and inventorying the sacristy; or doing other time-consuming and infrequent jobs that are accomplished pleasantly in fellowship and quickly when many hands share the work. While working, some altar guilds wear smocks or aprons or even head coverings for protection and for the anonymity uniforms bestow. Most altar guild workers are aware of the fund of information about housekeeping (stain removal, metal and wood care, for example), which is readily available from books, government pamphlets and the files of diocesan altar guilds. Hints for homemakers are also hints for church housekeepers. (Several suggestions for the care of specific church furnishings—candles, vessels, linens, vestments—are incorporated into the appropriate sections of this book and Appendix IV contains stain removal suggestions.)

Each altar guild has to establish its own housekeeping system and its own work schedule. Each also has to make up its own list of specific cleaning tasks to be done for each worship occasion, determined by the place it is making ready and the priest with whom it works, giving consideration to the time and schedule of the verger/sexton. No two churches have identical equipment or staff and no two altar guilds approach identical sets of tasks, so a standard list of cleaning procedures for all altar workers is pointless. Any system is acceptable as long as all the workers in one parish understand what is to be done before each service and how the assignments are to be handled. Any system is acceptable as long as it works well and produces a clean place for worship. Cleanliness comes first. After cleanliness comes decorating, setting the Table and preparing the vestments.

An essential part of the housekeeping for a celebration is picking up afterward. Picking up includes cleaning all the things that have been used and putting them away, straightening the furniture, restoring order to sanctuary, chancel and sacristy. Careful attention to these tasks lightens the obligation of altar guild workers arriving to prepare for subsequent services.

Decorating

Most parishes today are in the position of using, replacing or replenishing already existing supplies of ornaments and other furnishings rather than starting fresh. Perched between yesterday and tomorrow psychologically as well as practically, they are constantly weighing their old ways against the Church's new ones. Hangings of various kinds, candles, flowers, crosses and service books are the familiar ornaments used for enhancing the worship place. Styles change, customs come and go, art objects appear and disappear, but these familiar ornaments, new or old in design and material, are the ones altar guild workers still reach for first when decorating—using contemporary additions that seem artistically appropriate as they come along. In making decisions about decorating worship centers, whether indoors or outdoors, the question is no longer what must be done, but what can be done to make the place beautiful, to make it "a sanctuary, that the Lord may dwell among them" (Ex. 25:8).

Hangings—(Antependia, Paraments)

In the early centuries of the Church the altar represented Christ in the midst of his people and it was treated accordingly as the center of attention. A silk cloth draped it on all sides like a pall, the ancester of today's Jacobean frontal. Nothing else was placed on it except the linen cloth for the Eucharist, the cup, the bread and the Gospel book. In the time the silk cloth was decorated with embroidery and jewels and became quite elegant. Tapestry, damask, and brocade were introduced and colors were strong—typically red—in order to draw attention to the center of worship.

When the altar was lengthened in the Middle Ages and pushed against the wall, the draped "pall" could no longer be used, so the frontal and frontlet developed. These hangings covered the visible side of the altar only. Frontals were also made of rich material and they, too, became elaborate with orphreys, braid, fringe and embroidered emblems.

The familiar hangings of this century are descendants of these two, and modern adaptations are related. Frontals, superfrontals/frontlets, altar stoles and Laudean (Jacobean) frontals, made usually of richly-colored tapestries or brocade or substantial contemporary fabrics in various colors, provide a focal point for worshipers. The altar is meant to be visibly central, wherever it is, and lovely hangings are a convenient and appropriate means of making it so. Sometimes omitting the hangings (since they aren't required) can draw attention to the simple beauty of the wood or stone of the altar and let it speak for itself.

When new hangings are called for is it important to remember that anyone with a talent for sewing may make them by hand or by machine. They do not have to be "professionally" or commercially made. Amateurs have produced many gorgeous ones using all sorts of skills in stitchery, even spinning and weaving. All hangings may be made of any beautiful material suited to the purpose. They do not have to be made of traditional church fabric or in a seasonal color or in a standard shape or design. Texture, shape, color and design are best chosen to blend with the architecture and existing decor of the building where they will hang because, like everything else used to decorate a church, hangings provide background for worship. When they draw undue attention, they cease to be background. The current look in hangings is vibrant, simple and strong in keeping with cele-bration. The traditional look has intricate stitchery and ornate design, gold braid and fringe on rich dark colors, and is still desirable for some churches. Hangings may of course be purchased from church supply houses ready-made or made to order (and amply illustrated cata-logues provide an excellent guide to what is available). But today throughout the Church there is a call to local artists and craftspeople to use their gifts to create hangings and other appointments for their own worship places.

The following are the usual hangings from which parish choices may be made when hangings are desired:

A **frontal** hangs floor length on one side of the altar. A **frontlet** or **superfrontal** hangs about ten inches. They hang separately or together (the frontlet on top) and are made of material that drapes well. The frontlet may or may not be attached to the frontal. They are frequently but not always decorated with emblems, fringe or orphreys (wide appliquéd strips of other material), and are one color (not necessarily seasonal), multi-colored or neutral. Either type is usually hooked to the front of the altar or suspended from a piece of heavy white or off-white material, originally linen, the size of

FRONTALS (ANTEPENDIA)

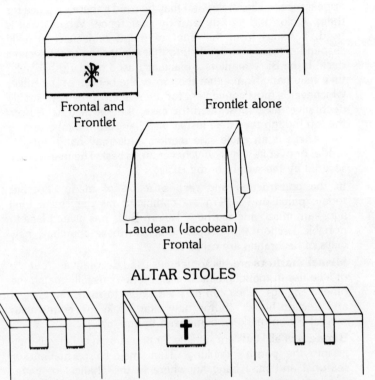

Frontal and
Frontlet

Frontlet alone

Laudean (Jacobean)
Frontal

ALTAR STOLES

the altar top (the *mensa*), kept in place in a way determined by the altar construction (hooks or a heavy metal bar encased in the top, for example).

Altar stoles (occasionally called frontlets) are strips of material like that used for frontals. They hang from the front of the altar, or from both front and back, about three-fourths of the distance to the floor. They may be attached to a white top-piece or lie across the altar. They may be of any width, are often decorated, and may be used singly or in pairs.

A **Laudean** (Jacobean) **frontal** hangs to the floor on all four sides of a free-standing altar. The top is white or off-white. This frontal drapes gracefully at the corners, but the fullness needs to be controlled so those moving about the altar won't trip. A Laudean type of frontal is also made with three sides for altars that stand against the wall. Laudean frontals are frequently multicolored or made in a color to harmonize with the decor of the church in order to be suitable for any occasion.

Pulpit or **lectern falls** and **Bible markers** are similar in appearance to altar stoles and may be used if there's a place for them. Color and size depend on preference. When a fall is used, it hangs from the front of pulpit or lectern, usually suspended from a piece of cloth that is attached to the lectern desk. If the Bible markers are actually used to mark the Bible, they may hang from either the top or the bottom of the Bible, whichever is most convenient for the reader. If they are strictly decorative, as is most often the case, they usually hang from the top though they may just as well hang from the bottom. If the lectern is an eagle, the marker ends may hang outside, inside, or over its wings, whichever looks best. The markers are secured by the weight of the Bible.

In the construction and reconstruction of many churches today, pulpit and lectern are combined (as they were long ago—an *ambo*) and the huge lectern Bible has given place to portable Lection and Gospel books. In these churches, new ways of decorating are called for.

Missal markers are still sometimes used decoratively, but are of little use in marking altar books. Markers usually match the other hangings. They can be used singly to mark the Gospel and Lection books. (Some new altar books are bound with several ribbon markers, some with thumb tabs.)

Banners of all kinds are suitable for any church building if they fit into the parish's thinking. They may be permanent or seasonal and may hang anywhere in the chancel or nave. Banners are a teaching device so are equally suitable for feasts or fasts. Very effective ones have been created for Lent and even for Good Friday.

Dossals and **riddels** are permanent decorative curtains hung to provide a backdrop for altars placed against a blank wall. They may be simple or ornate. The dossal is a full drape, usually of heavy material and rich color; it hangs on the wall behind the altar or on a frame attached to the back of the altar. Riddels are tall side curtains hanging from swinging bars attached to the ends of the altar or to the wall behind it.

A **funeral pall** is a hanging for a casket. It can be made of any material, any color, any design, simple or elaborate, and is large enough to cover the casket completely, beautiful enough to preclude the desire to decorate the casket with flowers. At one time palls were black, later purple or red, sometimes gold, usually white for children. Palls today tend to be white in keeping with the fact that "The liturgy for the dead is an Easter liturgy. It finds all its meaning in the resurrection . . . (and) is characterized by joy" (p. 507). A pall for a child's casket is sized accordingly. A silk chalice veil can conveniently be used as a pall for an urn of ashes. A flag is an acceptable hanging for the casket of a member of the armed forces.

The **Lenten Array** is an assortment of unbleached linen, muslin, homespun, or other rough cloth cut to sizes appropriate for covering church furnishings during Lent. The linen is often banded in dark red or otherwise simply decorated with dark red symbols of the Crucifixion. The custom of using Lenten Array is Anglican, dating back to the time of Edward VI, and many Episcopal churches are adopting it today. The altar, pulpit, lectern, pictures and crosses (except for a crucifix) all are covered, and the priest's vestments usually match. (A dossal, if there is one, usually matches.)

Many churches which do not use the Lenten Array follow the custom of veiling crosses and pictures in the church during Holy Week. Two color customs currently exist: purple veils from Palm Sunday to Maundy Thursday morning, white for the Maundy Thursday liturgy and black for Good Friday; or dark red (ox blood) for Palm Sunday and all of Holy Week. Either custom is appropriate but red is in keeping with the new church calendar.

Candles

Although candles at the altar are one of the expectations of worshipers, altar candles are not required by rubric. Rubrics for the Easter Vigil (p. 294) and the Order for Worship for Evening (p. 143) (services which are built around the lighting of candles) assume candles "at the altar" are waiting to be lighted, but nowhere in the Prayer Book are altar candles prescribed. In fact, except in those two candle-lighting services, in the service for the Dedication of a Church (pp. 574, 576) and in reference to the Paschal candle at burial and baptism (pp. 467, 313) and to a baptismal candle (p. 313), the rubrics do not mention candles. Altar workers follow Church and parish customs as well as artistic sense and good judgment in placing candles in the church. Guidance can also come from the priest or from books describing contemporary conduct of worship (including these few rubrics in the Prayer Book).

Torches, lamps and candles were incorporated into Christian worship as long ago as the fourth century. Torches were carried before a bishop in procession as a mark of dignity (just as they were carried before civil magistrates in Rome). Lamps and candles were hung over the altar or placed around it—sometimes for light, sometimes as tokens of joy and festivity. With few exceptions, no candles were put on the altar in the West or in the East until late in the twelfth century. Once the custom began, however, it spread throughout the Christian world and the number of candles on altars multiplied and varied. Records of English churches in the Middle Ages show nearly every number from one to twenty, but in the sixteenth century an injunction of Edward VI and several other rulings led to the tradition of two altar candles that is familiar (but not universal) in the Church of England and the Episcopal Church today. In the first years of the Episcopal Church, candles and other ornaments were not common, probably because of the subsistence economy of the colonies and the general feeling about religious simplicity. In the late nineteenth century, however, ornaments began to appear and since then there has been little question about using candles. They are used because they are festive and because they symbolize Christ, the Light of the World. In order to be festive and symbolic they have to be burning. Unlighted candles serve no more purpose in candle holders than they do in boxes, so it is appropriate in church as at home that they be out of sight unless they are to be lighted. Inclusion of candles in decoration involves the intention to light them.

Candle holders come in all shapes, sizes and materials. Altar workers need not be bound by traditional models stored in sacristies or pictured in catalogues. The holder that fits the place where the candle is needed and blends into the background is the one to use on a given occasion. It may be the church's fifty-year-old seven-branched candelabra or it may be a new pair of glass candlesticks borrowed from a parishioner. Candleholders are utilitarian: gold, silver, brass, iron, bronze, pewter, plate, pottery, wood, stone, glass or plastic; high, low, wide, thin, multiple or single. If they fit, they fit. Good taste will recognize beauty, match suitability to purpose and dictate artistic rightness.

Choice of candles to use in a particular parish depends on the occasion, tradition, equipment on hand, architecture, available space and other similar variables, not the least of which is the funds available to buy them. Candles are expensive. Shape, size, content and color have to be considered too. Any number of any type in any color in any kind of holder may be used for any service as long as the priest approves and they will add to and not detract from the Liturgy.

Candles that are traditional for one parish may not be for another. The following list is intended to indicate variety and explain terms for candles that the Church today has inherited. The list is not meant to suggest requirements.

Single candlesticks and **processional torches** are self-explanatory. They may be used in any multiple anywhere in the church according to the priest's direction and parish tradition.

Eucharistic candles is a term commonly used for the two or more candles placed on the altar. "Altar candles" are perhaps a more accurate term for them, because torches or pavement candles beside the altar may serve as lights for the Eucharist and any candles on the altar may be burned for any service. "Eucharistic candles" are lights for the Eucharist. In some churches where altar candles are lighted only for the Eucharist, they are not put in place until the Table is set at the Offertory and are removed after the Communion when the Table is cleared, therefore being termed Eucharistic candles. A parish practice depends on the priest. Altar candles may be any size—tall or short, wide or slender, determined by the size of the holder.

Office lights are candles placed behind or beside the altar with the intention of originally lighting them for Daily Morning or Evening Prayer (the "Office"). Since these candles do not have to be lighted for the Office and may on the other hand be lighted for any service at all, the placement, not the use, makes them "office lights" today. Single candles alone or in groups, candelabra or pavement lights may serve the purpose. Office lights are not required for Morning or Evening Prayer.

Pavement Lights are single, tall candles that usually stand on the floor of the sanctuary (the pavement) although they may stand anywhere in the chancel. Probably they originated from the two candles carried in processions in the early Church and then used for reading lights.

Candelabra are branched candlesticks, usually designed for three, five or seven candles and can be styled either to stand on the floor or be placed on a table.

The **Paschal Candle** is a tall (thirty-plus inches), sometimes decorated candle, lighted with the new fire at the Easter Vigil (p. 285) and burned (p. 287) during every service in the church from Easter to Pentecost. The Paschal candle may stand at the font for the rest of the year. It is the source of light for baptismal candles (p. 313), may be carried at the head of funeral processions (p. 467) and is sometimes used as the Christ candle in the center of the Advent wreath.

The **Advent wreath** is a circular candle holder for four or five candles, four for the four Sundays in Advent with a Christ candle in the center, if desired. The Christ candle is white, the other four may be white, blue, purple, a combination of three purple and one pink (for Gaudete Sunday, the third Sunday in Advent, a happy day) or any other color suitable to the place. The candles are lighted progressively, one on the first Sunday, two on the second, until all five are burning on Christmas Eve. The wreath may be of any material, simple or ornate, and may be hung or placed on a stand of some kind. It is sometimes decorated with greens which are treated to comply with fire regulations. (Laurel is safer than conifers.)

Sanctuary lights (sometimes called vigil lights) are candles of different shapes and sizes, usually encased in glass chimneys for long term burning. Originally, sanctuary lights were the several lamps hung across the sanctuary to light the altar. Eventually they came to signify God's presence in the church. From this significance grew the practice of burning one night and day in front of the aumbry (a wall safe, usually in the sanctuary) or the tabernacle (a locked box on the altar) in which the Sacrament is reserved.

Miscellaneous notes about candles:

Traditionally candles have been made of 51 percent to 100 percent beeswax. This was the earliest candle material and is of course pure (or nearly pure), hence its significance for use. Stearine candles are less expensive and are satisfactory, if an altar guild prefers to use them. Candles are ordered by diameter and length, not purpose. Established church supply houses will understand church requirements better than general candle suppliers, but ordering by size is still generally necessary. All churches don't use the same size for one purpose. Tall thick candles last longer and from a distance look sturdier than thin ones.

Candles harden with age. Older candles burn longer. If they are ordered in quantity to allow aging, they have to be kept in a cool place, the cooler the better.

Candles can be cleaned easily with alcohol or with a little salad oil on a very soft cloth and shined with a piece of nylon stocking.

Cleaning candle holders depends on material. Rinsing in very hot water and wiping with paper towels is effective in most instances except on lacquered metal. (See Appendix IV, removing wax stains.) Too much polishing is not good for brass or silver according to reliable metal workers. Polishing two or three times a year is sufficient, maintaining shine in the interim by rubbing with a soft cloth or treated polishing gloves.

Followers (glass, brass or chrome cylinders made to fit over the candle tops) prevent drips, prolong the life of candles and keep flames even. They may be ordered from church supply houses by candle diameter. It is easy to keep them free from wax build-up by rinsing them regularly with very hot water and wiping them with paper towels. (When working with wax, use a separate basin to avoid pouring waxy water down the drain.)

Bobêches (bō besh or bō bāsh—only two syllables whether singular or plural) are glass or plastic collars for candles or candle sockets which catch drips. They are cleaned with hot water, ammonia and paper towels, using a separate basin.

Candle extinguishers need regular cleaning too. Any soot accumulation in the bell top is potentially hazardous to linens, rugs and floors. Soot can be removed with hot water and paper towels, again using a separate basin.

Wax **tapers** need frequent trimming to remove frayed ends. New candle wicks will be easier for acolytes to light and less likely to sputter out if they are lighted for a few minutes when new.

Long candle wicks need trimming to prevent charred ends breaking off and soiling linens. Short wicks require a little candle carving to facilitate lighting.

Candle tubes and **candle joiners** both continue the life of candles. White, offwhite or colored tubes hold stubs or broken, mismatched or misshapen candles on a spring base that feeds them to the top and allows them to burn to the last flicker. Joiners are couplers, usually metal, for two candle stubs which allow the top one to burn an extra few inches. Both tubes and couplers are available at most church supply houses.

Candle stubs tend to collect in sacristies. Some altar guild workers melt these down to make new altar candles, Paschal Candles, sanctuary lights or Christmas candles. Some religious orders accept candle stubs (as a gift) for the same purpose. Some candle manufacturers buy back their own candle refuse. Finding a way to dispose of candle stubs usefully is good church housekeeping.

Flowers

Flowers are an extra. They aren't necessary in church, but when they appear they provide a finishing touch to an already beautiful scene. Flowers speak of festivity. In fact the only rubric in the entire Prayer Book that even mentions them refers to a festive occasion—

the Dedication and Consecration of a Church (p. 574). In that service "as the furnishings of the church are dedicated, they may be decorated by members of the congregation with flowers . . ."—including the altar, by implication, because the altar will be dedicated. For hundreds of years flowers have decked churches for festivals, but apparently not altars, if pictures and records of early times are accurate. Not until the late nineteenth century did flowers become generally acceptable decorations "on or above the Table" in either the Church of England or the Episcopal Church,[7] and even then they weren't required. Worshipers today consider flowers at the altar normal and expect them elsewhere in the church on special occasions. In fact, people are so accustomed to seeing flowers in church that they are quite likely to note their absence (except perhaps during Advent or Lent).

With a minimum of practice anyone can arrange flowers for the altar. Learning comes from doing and from acceptance of the effort. A little knowledge about flowers, some common sense and a feeling about overall effective decoration—the beauty of the whole instead of the parts—will guide most people through creating a flower arrangement. Some are quicker at learning and more clever at doing than others, but anyone can make an acceptable offering. The flowers are a gift of life and love presented to God, not to the congregation.

Flower arranging for a church is not a competition and flower show standards of form, distribution and content don't apply. Altar guild arrangers need not feel restricted by the expectations of others or burdened by numerous ideas people have about "proper" arrangements. Basic knowledge about flowers can be obtained from books on flowers and flower arranging (fresh and dried), books that are practical rather than arty or professional.[8] The common sense about arranging comes from experience. The feeling about effective decoration comes from observation. The only standard for church arrangements is that flowers at the altar or in any other area blend into the background of the worship center and increase its beauty.

What is "appropriate" is whatever natural materials can be made attractive at a given time for a given situation. Any real flowers are appropriate—garden, greenhouse, field or woods, even the blossoms that people call weeds. The rest of God's creation is appropriate too—leaves and branches, greens and grasses, nuts and berries, vegetables and fruits, pods and tassels. Dried flowers, potted plants and trees are appropriate if they fit the occasion. All of these speak of life at one stage or another; on the altar they are a gift of life. In the past, it has not been customary to use even the most exquisite artificial flowers for the altar because they represent life only symbolically. They aren't life; they aren't God's gift returned to him. If the suggestion of using artificial flowers arises, the priest decides.

Any container is appropriate, if it holds the flowers of the day well and if it is clean. (The suggestions for cleaning candle holders also apply to flower containers.) A container may be an ancient brass vase from the sacristy or any receptacle of a useful shape that will hold water. An arrangement of any design is appropriate if it fits the space nicely. Any color is appropriate for any season. Any number of blossoms is appropriate. Symmetry is appropriate and so is asymmetry if it is effective.

In many parishes altar flower committees have always gathered their own floral materials from the world around them and have consequently never faced a problem of insufficient funds if working with a tight budget. In other parishes, where the custom of memorial prayers on specific Sundays has long been tied to contributions for that Sunday's flowers, altar guilds constantly face this problem. The difficulty in these parishes for priests and altar guilds alike lies in helping donors dissociate money contributed from prayers offered and from flowers used on specific Sundays. Some parishes have changed to revolving flower funds to which contributions may be made and from which flowers may be purchased. Other parishes have promoted "living memorials" to honor loved ones, using contributions to help with the needs of people in the parish, for example, and freeing flower arrangers to gather materials for arrangements as they see fit. (The prayers for special occasions and people become a separate matter under these circumstances, handled independently of flowers.)

The whole purpose of flowers is to add beauty to the church, not to dominate, not to distract and not to obstruct the worship that is taking place. For that reason, it is customary to discourage a profusion of flowers at the front of the church at weddings, funerals or other special services, limiting those occasions to the usual arrangements at the altar, if possible. When extra flowers are given at these times, they can be placed at the entrance or in some spot where they will add to the joyous spirit but not be center stage. If questions are asked, altar guild members can often be very helpful in explaining the reasons.

In some parishes regular altar guild workers manage all the steps of floral decoration. In other parishes, a flower committee is in charge and is responsible to the altar guild leader and the priest. In either situation the group responsible needs to understand the purpose of flowers in the church and all the possibilities open to it in placing them there. As a rule, professional flower people, such as florists, decorators, bridal consultants, are not invited to help because they usually lack the liturgical background for this understanding. As long as the people working with flowers have the priest's blessing, they are free to try almost anything at the altar and around the church, from indoor gardens of spring flowers at Easter (representing the garden at the tomb) to the "holly and ivy, box and bay, put in the church on Christmas Day" as a symbol of the new life and joy brought by the Christ Child. Each church lends itself to imaginative ideas for decorating. Arrangements in the sanctuary are hardly the limit of what can be done to make the building come alive with flowers. Finding unexpected places to add touches of beauty is a challenge.

Other Furnishings

Other items entrusted to the custody of altar workers vary according to parish possessions, but all the furnishings that have to do with any worship in a parish qualify. Altar workers are responsible for their care, storage and timely appearance. The following list contains items common to most churches; each parish will have its own additions.

The **Altar Book (Missal)** containing the Holy Eucharist, the **Gospel Book**, the **Lection Book** containing Lessons and Epistles grouped according to the Prayer Book Lectionary, and the great **Lectern Bible**. (The rubric, p. 406: "It is desirable that the Lessons and Gospel be read from a book or books of appropriate size and dignity.")

The **Missal Stand** (brass, wood or other metal) or **Missal Pillow** (more suitably used on free standing altars) on which the Altar Book may rest during the Eucharist.

The **Alms Basins** (not "offering plates" or "collection plates") and the **Receiving Basin** (for the several small basins). Bason is simply an old spelling of this word, not a special term.

The **Processional Cross** and other crosses, standing or hanging. Names and descriptions of different types can be found in most books on church symbols.

The **Wedding Pillows** or kneelers (sometimes one long one), often white and decorated, for the bride and groom to kneel on during the marriage service.

A **Christmas Creche.**

All furnishings in the church are part of the centers of worship—altars, pulpit and lectern, or ambo (a podium), font, statues, pictures and litany desk, for example.

Setting the Table

Once the worship place is clean and suitably decorated with appropriate hangings, flowers, and candles, and the alms basins and books for the service are in place according to the priest's directions, it is time to focus on the Table and the dishes and linens for the feast.

In the early years of the Church, Christian Jews met in each other's homes to break bread together following their regular Friday night gathering in the synagogue for reading from the Scripture, teaching, prayers and a final Shalom—"The Peace of the Lord"—before separating. When they began meeting in public buildings after Constantine made Christianity legal in the fourth century, their ceremony of setting the Table for celebrating the feast with their Lord was modeled after the ceremony of that simple home meal of the early days. The Table was bare until after the proclamation of the Word (the readings from Scripture, the teaching and the prayers) which took place in a large room where everyone could gather around an ambo (a podium). Then the people exchanged the familiar greeting of Peace and moved to the Table where they presented their gifts for the feast to deacons who placed them on the Table. A procession developed around this movement from one part of the building to the other. The candles of the procession became the candles of the Table and the linen, the cup, the bread and the wine were also carried to the Table by the worshipers. The Table was set with simplicity.

In succeeding years, hangings, candles, linens and vessels made of silver, gold and other rich materials were added in abundance to that simply set Table. Eventually the importance of the furnishings overshadowed the importance of the Table itself. For the last fifty years, the Church has been gradually returning to its beginnings when the Table was bare until the Offertory procession and then set with simplicity.[9]

It is not necessary for the Tables of the Church to be always set in the same way any more than it is necessary for the buildings to be decorated in the same way or the participants to be dressed in the same way. Today church people, especially those who plan the services, are beginning to see the place of variety in worship experience and to enjoy the opportunity to express their differences.

Priests are free to plan the worship for their own parishes using either Rite I or Rite II, involving as much of the congregation in the planning as seems practical (an altar guild, a worship or liturgical committee) and staying within the framework of the rubrics, the Bishop's guidance and a sensitivity to parish traditions. Every parish has always had individual worship traditions—its own look, its own atmosphere, its own ceremonial. Considering those traditions in planning is important. Changing tradition at times is also important, because it is not always rubrical and often it can hold back a congregation with specifics so that its freedom in worship is stifled.

The priest of a parish, often working with a worship committee, decides on the way to conduct the Eucharist in that parish for each occasion. In the course of time, there are many ways for many occasions. In the spirit of the Prayer Book, no one way is intended to be the only way as long as the Eucharist remains "the principal act of Christian worship on the Lord's Day and other major Feasts" (p. 13). Nor is any one way preferred as long as "The Holy Table is spread with a clean white cloth during the celebration" (p. 406), and bread and wine are returned to God from the congregation at the Offertory (pp. 333, 361), placed on the Table by the deacon (pp. 322, 354, 407) (or an appropriate minister) with one cup for the wine "and, if need be, a flagon" (p.407), and offered by the priest with the words that Scripture says our Lord used at the Last Supper to be blessed, broken and given back as the Body and Blood of Christ. These rubrics for the feast allow great leeway to those making plans. The responsibility of altar guild workers is to devise practical methods for putting the plans into effect with reverence and beauty. The leeway makes it as impossible to give specific directions for arranging vessels and linens that will apply to altar guilds in all parishes at all times as it is to give specific directions for any other part of preparing a church for worship.

In general, the dishes and the linens that are to be used for the Eucharist are expected to be clean and in designated places at a pre-determined time and the bread and wine ready. An agreed upon procedure makes everyone comfortable and confident. Part of that procedure is having all preparations completed well before the service starts. Altar guild workers rushing around at the last minute disturb both the atmosphere of a church ready for worship and the meditations of worshipers who arrive early at service for a time of quiet.

If the Table is to be totally bare until the Offertory, someone has to spread the "clean white cloth" before the deacon can set the bread and cup on it. Someone also has to put the altar candles in place if they are to be used. The deacon, the servers, altar guild workers or members of the congregation can do this at the time of the Offertory before the presentation of the gifts. In many parishes the altar workers still spread the cloth before the service, or uncover the cloth and change it if it is not fresh. Frequently, they spread the corporal and place candles at the same time, although the candles sometimes remain unlighted until the Offertory.

Although the familiar vested chalice is still placed on the altar at the beginning of the service in some parishes, recognition of the historic significance of the bare Table before the Offertory and acceptance of the function of the deacon as table setter has led to a now frequent practice of placing the chalice vested or unvested on the credence or another side table in the sanctuary or leaving it in the sacristy until the Offertory. Then the deacon or a server fetches it. Another practice is to present the empty chalice, sometimes even the altar cloth, with the other gifts in the offertory procession—a practice reminiscent of ceremonial in the early Church. If the chalice is to be presented, it is placed with the bread and the wine on a table in the nave (see below).

Vesting the chalice was developed late in the life of the Church only for convenience. When vesting is the practice, the paten is nested in the bowl of the chalice (cushioned by a purificator to prevent scratches) for ease in carrying the two together. A priest's wafer may be placed on the paten. The stiff pall is placed on the paten as a form over which to drape the silk veil. The burse holds all the necessary small linens. In parishes where the priest still wishes to have the chalice vested in this manner, the following diagram will be useful.

A VESTED CHALICE

1. The Chalice
2. Purificator
3. The Paten
4. The Priest's Wafer (optional)
5. Linen Pall
6. Silk Veil
7. Burse

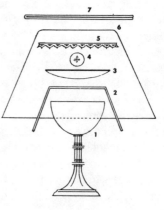

The credence table if possible is at the right of the priest standing at the altar, for that is the side of the deacon. In some sanctuaries where the credence is fixed to the east or south wall and the altar has been moved out to be free standing, ceremonial has to be adjusted or a new credence arrangement devised.

Because the bread and wine are now presented in procession, setting the credence is simpler than it once was. It is set to be convenient for the people using it. It may be covered with a white cloth. A small bottle, cruet or pitcher of water is placed on it as well as a lavabo and towel, if they are used. Extra chalice or two is necessary for chalice bearers and possibly small bowls, baskets or plates for concelebrants to use in serving the Bread. In parishes where the chalice is no longer vested, the empty chalice covered with a purificator to keep it clean may be placed on the credence until the Offertory, as noted above and the small linens may be placed on the credence in a neat pile. This can include extra purificators and two corporals, one to be spread on the Table, the other to be placed over any remnants of the Sacrament after the Communion. These linens may be placed in the burse instead (even though the chalice is no longer vested) and the burse laid or stood on the credence.

Whether wafers or real bread is the bread of the Feast, the priest's and the people's offering is one. All the bread is the whole gift of the whole community and is presented in one container. When a loaf of bread is used, whatever its size or shape, the unity is obvious, but when wafers are used, thinking has to stretch to encompass presenting the large wafer (which has so long been a separate bread) with the small ones. When the bread presented is wafers, the priest breaks the large wafer at the fraction and divides the small ones among the plates of any concelebrants who will assist in serving. Some parishes are using only priest's hosts which are all broken and shared. When the bread presented is a loaf, the priest breaks it at the fraction, then breaks it into enough smaller sections for concelebrants or sometimes for the people to use as ministers of the Sacrament to each other.

The bread and the wine for the Offertory are placed on a table in the nave located where all the people can see their offering. The location depends on the building. It may be near the entrance; it may be in the midst of the center aisle. A white cloth may cover this table. In some churches a lighted candle is placed on it to be extinguished when the bread and wine are taken to the altar. In some parishes communicants arriving for the service break pieces from the loaf themselves (or take individual wafers from a container) and place them in the bowl or basket used for presentation. In some parishes the bread and wine are provided by different people from the community each week and these people present the gifts themselves at the Offertory on behalf of the whole community, sometimes keeping them in the pew until that time and sometimes placing them on the nave table.

The wine is presented in a cruet, a flagon, a beaker, a pitcher, a decanter, a bottle, or some other container that is large enough to accommodate the expected number of communicants. Although only one chalice is on the altar during the prayer of consecration, all the wine for the Feast is consecrated at the same time. Extra chalices are filled after the Breaking of the Bread for all the chalice bearers or for the people to use if the practice is for them to administer the chalice to each other.

After the service, the altar candles are commonly removed from the Table and the white cloth either removed and put away or covered with a protector to keep it clean. The dishes and the soiled linens are washed and put away. Vessels and linens which have been used with the consecrated bread and wine are rinsed before washing, either in a piscina which drains into the ground or in a bowl of water which is then emptied onto the ground.

Priests have different instructions about the remnants of the Sacrament. According to the rubric (p.409) "the celebrant or deacon, or other communicants, reverently eat and drink it, either after the Communion of the people or after the Dismissal." In some parishes the priest does the ablutions at the altar at some point after the communion and consumes the remnants at that time. In other parishes, the Table is cleared immediately after the Communion by the deacon or server. The vessels and the remnants covered with a corporal are placed on the credence or in the sacristy and reverently taken care of later as the priest directs. Remnants of the consecrated bread and wine are always either reserved or consumed, but leavened bread should be consumed because it does not store well.

The rest of the cleaning up, as has already been indicated, consists of restoring complete order to the sanctuary and any other worship areas that the service has involved, as well as the sacristy. Everything that has been used is put away. Flowers may be bundled for delivery according to parish custom. The furniture is straightened and the floor swept if necessary. Altar guild workers leave the church building in a condition in which they would be glad to find it if they were arriving to start their work.

The obligation of the priest of a parish church to those who prepare its altar is obvious. Enabling them to carry out their ministry well requires more than simple instruction. Real teaching has to take place. It is important for altar workers to know the reasons for what they do and to have a grasp of the entire liturgy for which they are preparing.

Bread and Wine

The bread of the Eucharist has alternated between real bread, leavened and unleavened, and paper-thin wafers since the Middle Ages. Wafers were first introduced at that time, together with other related ceremonial changes, as a way to protect the Sacrament from abuse, particularly from being fragmented and taken from the Church for private and superstitious use. Early prayer books of the English Church "specified that the wafers (then being used) be larger and thicker than before and that each was to be broken into two or more pieces" and again that "the best wheat bread was sufficient." In the Episcopal Church wafers appeared in place of bread in the eighteenth century and became customary until the gradual return to real bread that has been taking place in the last half of the twentieth century.[10]

Wafers in the United States have traditionally been handmade by sisters in several Episcopal convents. Although some church supply houses offer wafers for sale, their product does not carry the idea of "hand-made for the Lord's service." With the return of real bread to the Table, "hand-made" moves closer to the parish. The talents of parishioners are frequently called upon to make it, altar workers included. Today loaves of bread of all shapes, sizes and derivation appear on the altar including eastern and western, leavened and unleavened, plain and sweet, white and brown. The use of real bread sometimes results in a problem with crumbs, but priests have discovered that mid-east bread (pita) will tear into many pieces easily and makes practically no crumbs. Pita bread is not at all difficult to make, it keeps well when frozen, and it is thin enough for two loaves to be broken together at the fraction if many people are to share it.[11]

The wine of the Eucharist in the early Church was red, the common wine of the people. Although it has been white or golden in some eras since, it is again red in most churches today. Any wine can be the wine for the Table, commercial or home-made, sweet or dry. One of the altar guild's responsibilities is to be sure the supply of wine (and bread) is always ample. Even when both are supplied by parishioners at the time of the service, a reserve supply in the sacristy is good practice in case of emergency.

Bread and wine have been associated with religious meals and ceremonies—the heart of a people's Being—from as far back as we have knowledge of these things. Although the Christian Eucharist has its direct origin in the Passover meal of its Jewish heritage, its roots lie in the earliest practices of human beings at worship. Bread is the mainstay of mankind, "the staff of life," the most basic example of what God's people have made from his most necessary gift, the grain. At the offertory the people present this bread to him, the symbol of his gift of their life and work on earth. He blesses and returns it to them as the Bread of Heaven, the symbol of his gift of life redeemed, the body of our Lord Jesus Christ. They present the wine which they have made from his gift of fruit, wine which bubbles with life of its own. They offer it as a symbol of joy and fellowship and fullness of life on earth, and it too he blesses and gives back as the bonding, life-giving blood of Christ.[12]

The Vessels

Chalice

The chalice or cup holds the wine mixed with water for consecration and administration to the people. Traditionally it has been about eight to twelve inches tall, footed, with a plain or decorated knob (knop, knurl) on the stem as an aid in holding it firm. It has commonly been silver or gold, sometimes simple, sometimes exquisitely crafted with filigree and jewels. Chalices like this are still available, but today others in many shapes, sizes and materials are also available such as pottery, stone, glass, pewter and ceramic. Any kind or size of cup suitable to the group, the occasion, and the place is appropriate, though it is desirable to seek excellence in workmanship and to use a cup large enough to be seen by everyone present when it is on the Table. Most parishes have at least one extra chalice for an emergency or for a concelebrant to use.

Paten

The paten is the plate that holds the bread for consecration and administration. Traditionally it has been matched to the chalice in pattern because of the custom of nesting it on the bowl of the chalice before and after the service. It does not have to match, however, nor does it have to be nested even when it does match. Today patens are as varied as chalices. A single parish may use different patens according to the type of bread used at the Eucharist. A large plate, a platter, a bowl or a basket is more useful for a loaf of bread or for sections of a loaf than the six- or seven-inch paten customarily used for wafers. This larger container would hold the loaf both for the Offertory procession and for the consecration. The paten is no longer mentioned in the rubrics of the prayer of consecration. The priest holds the bread itself or lays a hand on it. It is possible to break the bread and serve it without using any kind of plate. Many parishes have small extra bread containers for concelebrants to use.

Flagon, Pitcher

The rubric (p. 407) "it is appropriate that there be only one chalice on the altar" mentions a flagon for extra wine from which to fill other chalices after the prayer of consecration. A flagon is an over-size cruet, holding approximately a quart. Shape, material and size are a matter of preference. A pitcher, a decanter, a bottle or any other similar container may hold the wine of the offering in place of a flagon.

Ciborium Bread Box

The use of these two vessels depends on local practice. Both containers are designed to hold wafers and will not conveniently hold real bread. A ciborium is similar to a chalice, but has a cover usually with a standing cross on top for a handle. A bread box has no standard shape, size or design. A parish using bread has no need for either except perhaps for reservation of wafers for the sick (because leavened bread cannot be successfully reserved). Both vessels have traditionally been silver or gold, often matched to the rest of the silver or gold vessels, but both may be of any other material suitable for the purpose such as wood, glass, pewter or earthenware.

Cruets

Two cruets, one for wine and one for water, have been usual for preparing the chalice before the prayer of consecration. Size, material and shape depend on local requirements and preference. Cruets need not match the chalice and paten. They need not even match each other, nor do they both have to be used in a service. An average-sized water cruet may be a convenient container for the water which is placed on the credence, but an average-sized wine cruet may not be large enough for the wine of the offering. If that is the case, a flagon or some other larger container can take its place on the table in the nave.

Lavabo

A lavabo is a small bowl used in some churches for a ceremonial washing of the priest's fingers before the Great Thanksgiving. When used, the bowl (with a towel) is placed on the credence. Shape, size and material are a matter of preference. The lavabo ceremony is ancient, originating at the time when priests received all sorts of gifts from the people at the Offertory and really needed to wash their hands before blessing and breaking the bread. Reciting Psalm 26:6 was part of the ceremony: "I will wash my hands in innocence . . ." Today many priests no longer practice this ceremonial.

The Priest's Communion Kit

Many parishes or priests have a set of miniature Eucharistic vessels, commonly silver or silver plate but often of some other material. A kit usually contains a chalice, a paten, a bread box and cruets and sometimes a cross, candlesticks and a spoon, the essentials for setting a miniature altar for a private Communion. (Miniature linens to go with it can be made or purchased.) Marion Hatchett suggests avoiding doll-sized sets if possible "for they trivialize the sacrament."[13]

Pyx

A pyx is a box the size of a watch case but deeper, usually silver or gold, used for carrying the Blessed Sacrament to the sick. It often has a leather or cloth case with an attached cord or chain so it can be worn around the neck.

Oil Stock

A stock is a small screw-top cylindrical container for carrying the anointing oils. Stocks are available with more than one compartment for keeping the oils for different purposes separate.

Baptismal Bowl

If the font does not have a drain direct to the ground, it is customary to use an auxiliary bowl inside the font to hold the water of baptism (which can then be emptied on the ground). Although lovely Revere-shaped or footed silver bowls are often used for this purpose, a baptismal bowl may be of any material. A bowl is also used when a baptism takes place away from the font.

Shell

A shell is a shell-shaped scoop, usually silver, for spooning baptismal water on the head of the candidate. (A scallop shell is the symbol of baptism.) Use of a shell is optional: the priest's hand is as effective.

Ewer

A ewer is a large pitcher used for pouring the water for baptism into the font. Any large pitcher is suitable. Where a baptismal bowl is used in the font, the need for a ewer has been questioned because the bowl can be filled before it is put in place. Continued use of the ewer is probably wise, so that the water can be seen by all present.

Thurible (Censer), Boat and Spoon

The boat is the container for the incense which is spooned into the thurible and burned over charcoal. Several styles are available. Thurible, boat, spoon, charcoal, tongs and matches are generally stored in one place for the convenience of the thurifer (the censer bearer). The ceremonial use of incense in procession and in worship goes back in Christian liturgy to at least the sixth century. Through the years it has been used with varied significance, but today it is basically a symbol of prayer. Use is optional in the Episcopal Church. If directions are needed, they can be found in priest's manuals.

Sanctus Bell

A Sanctus Bell is sometimes a single bell, sometimes three or four. When one is used, it is placed on the floor at the Epistle end of the altar during the Eucharist and the server customarily rings it at the Sanctus, during the prayer of consecration, and at the priest's communion.

The many different styles of all these vessels are amply illustrated in standard church supply house catalogues, but these catalogues show for the most part silver, silver plate and gold, indicating only part of the variety of materials in use in the Church today. Vessels made of other metals, stone, ceramic, glass and earthenware have to be examined in the work of individual craftsmen and commercial establishments specializing in these materials.

CARING FOR VESSELS

If the vessels are made of material other than silver or gold, cleaning them is simple. Wash vessels in hot water and use a mild soap, rinse well, then dry with a soft dish towel, rubbing briskly to make the vessels shine. Good care includes storing vessels in plastic or cloth bags so they will stay clean between uses and keeping vessels in a place where they won't be easily broken.

Silver and gold vessels are also best cared for by the same method, using hot water and soap and a soft towel. Storage in bags made of Pacific cloth or some other tarnish retardant material is recommended. Silver lasts longer if polished infrequently, according to reputable silversmiths, and gold should be polished only by a goldsmith or a jeweler. Vessels set with precious or semi-precious stones require special attention because stones can chip or crack if water is too hot or if they are struck. Mountings need to be checked regularly and repaired by a reliable jeweler if loose. Chemical cleaners damage some stones, so warm water and soap is safest for washing all these vessels—using a soft brush for cleaning around the stones and a soft cloth for a final polish. Storing each in a separate bag is an added protection.

Altar guilds have overpolished for years, thereby unwittingly cutting short the life of the lovely vessels in their charge. Polishing with a reliable polish only two or three times a year is usually sufficient to keep silver pieces in immaculate condition if they are rubbed with a soft towel whenever they are washed. Polishing gloves impregnated with jeweler's rouge for maintaining shine between polishings and for rubbing away finger prints and other marks that soap and water doesn't eliminate are available in jewelry and department stores as well as gift shops. Cakes of camphor from the drugstore are a very effective tarnish retardant when kept in the closet or safe where the silver is stored.

An immovable fireproof safe in the sacristy or elsewhere in the building is an essential part of good vessel care. Even churches are not burglar proof or fire proof. In addition to the safe, a meticulous inventory of the church's valuable possessions is also essential. The inventory should be complete with a history, a professional appraisal, photographs and a full verbal description of all the distinguishing marks and characteristics of each piece. The inventory belongs in a safe deposit box or the church lawyer's office, not in the church building.

One of the concerns of altar guilds is that with the variations in tradition in a parish many of its lovely vessels and linens are no longer useful. Like lovely linens and dishes in many parish homes they sit on shelves to no purpose. Some of these might well be appreciated in other parts of the Church in parishes with other customs. Some of the oldest might be of interest to historical museums. In some parishes valuable articles no longer used have been sold and the money placed in a contemporary living memorial. Arranging for church vessels and linens to be put to dignified use somewhere is good stewardship.

Linens

LINENS IN GENERAL

The various white covers and cloths used on the altar and other tables and shelves in the sanctuary and sacristy during the Eucharist, baptism and all other services of the Church are known collectively as "linens." This does not mean that they are made of pure linen for they are often cotton or combinations of cotton or linen and synthetics. The term is a general one, used for convenience as household linens are called "linens," and it refers to fair linens, corporals, purificators, lavabo and baptismal towels, chalice (or stiff) palls, post-communion and aumbry veils, credence covers and covers for retable, shelves and incidental tables, cerecloths and protectors and dust covers (which may be colored instead of white). Although all these are the traditional church linens used and often made by altar guilds, none but the clean white cloth of the Prayer Book rubric (p. 408) is mandatory. All the others have been added through the years for appearance and practicality. When customs have changed, linens have changed also.

All church linens may be made of any firm white material that fits the requirements for the use of the article in terms of weight, weave and durability. Either pure material or synthetic is perfectly acceptable. Pure linen has been the fabric traditionally used but in the United States linen is imported, difficult to procure and very expensive, so both yardage and finished articles are often beyond parish budgets. The many other white goods available have proved suitable through experimental use, and altar guilds long familiar with the sewing, laundering and storage qualities of pure linen are now becoming familiar with those qualities of cottons, synthetics and combination fibers. These materials differ markedly, and they all differ from linen, so testing a sample according to its intended use before buying an appreciable quantity is important. There are questions to be considered. Is it easy to sew and embroider? Can common stains be completely removed? Does it maintain whiteness? Does it launder well? Is it fire resistant? Cotton in various weights which has been combined with polyester or treated to become "permanent press" is a popular choice because it meets these requirements and is considerably less expensive than linen.

Pure linen, the traditional material, comes in many widths and textures. The kind used for church linens is a fine weave, wide-width linen which is available in several weights. The medium weight is generally used for fair linens, corporals, stiff palls, towels and credence and other covers because it is firm. The light weight linen can be made into purificators and veils. Heavy linen, obtainable in textured as well as plain weave and in light blue or natural as well as white, is often used for protectors and the tops of frontals.

Sources of material sometimes overlooked are the linen closets in the sacristy and in parish homes. Unused, or no longer used but in good condition, plain white table cloths can be remade into small linens. Fine linen, cotton or lace handkerchiefs can be used as aumbry veils or miniature linens for a private communion set. Remnants from cutting standard sized linens are frequently the right size for these miniature sets as well as for stole protectors. White birdseye or fine huck or linen hand towels can be remade into baptismal, lavabo or sacristy towels and fine linen sheeting can be remade into any small linens, including fair linens for small altars. With the priest's permission the best parts of any worn larger church linens (including albs) may be cut out and remade into smaller ones. Embroideries can be removed from worn linens and appliquéd onto new ones (leaving a turn-under edge when cutting, using fine stitches and perhaps couching down, using perle cotton). Old lace pieces can be used as banding or edging or artistically arranged together on suitable background material for post-communion or aumbry veils, or even a festival frontal.[14]

Included in the following descriptions of the individual linens are directions for making them. The instructions are for average sizes and may be enlarged or reduced according to circumstances. Obviously in making linens the object in most cases is to cut the maximum number of pieces from standard width materials with a minimum of waste, so adjusting measurements to the yardage at hand within reason is practical. Specifications given here for hem widths are also average and may vary. Hems sewn with fine waxed cotton thread (thread drawn over the edge of a cake of beeswax, available at sewing centers) have added strength. Stitches should be fine and as close together as possible because wide-spaced stitches break apart during laundering. Fine needles help produce fine stitches.

LINENS IN PARTICULAR

Cerecloth

Traditionally a cerecloth covers a bare stone altar to protect the other linens from condensation. (A cerecloth is not needed on a wooden altar.) As its name implies, cerecloth was heavy waxed linen.

This waxed linen is no longer being manufactured but waterproof white flannelette is a satisfactory substitute and when used for this purpose can still be called a cerecloth. Waterproof cloth may also be placed over the frontal top under the fair linen as a buffer for wine stains. A cerecloth, either waxed linen or flannelette, is simply cut to size; it is not sewn.

Fair Linen

The fair linen is the "clean white cloth" of the rubric, used as the Table cover for the Eucharist. It is made of medium weight linen or other material. Although other cloths are usually placed under it, a fair linen may be used alone. It may fit the altar exactly or hang down on the ends or on all sides to any length. The cut size should allow for generous hems, one and a half to two inches, because good hems help the linen lie flat and hang straight. Corners are mitered. Embroidered crosses may mark the four corners and center of the altar top but are not necessary. The overhanging edges may be embroidered simply or elaborately in white or any appropriate color. They may also be edged with lace.

Protector, Dust Cover

A protector is placed over the fair linen between services to protect it. It is usually made of any nice material, white or colored, and may fit the altar top exactly or overhang to cover the fair linen completely. In some churches matching protectors in a color suitable to the church decor cover the main altar, side altars, credence and other table surfaces between services. In some churches because of unusual circumstances (excessive dust, for example) protectors are made of plastic or plasticized cloth. At one time in some churches the protector was always white and covered the fair linen during services other than the Eucharist. A protector for this purpose was sometimes called a prayer cloth, and in churches following this practice a second protector, often colored and usually called a dust cover, was placed over the prayer cloth between services. Dust cover today is commonly another term for a general protector; if a prayer cloth is used, it is called a prayer cloth.

Corporal

A corporal is a square of medium weight white fabric spread in the center of the fair linen during the Eucharist as an extra covering on which the vessels of the Eucharist used at the altar are placed. It protects the fair linen like a placemat and may have a square of

waterproof cloth under it. A second corporal may be used instead of
the chalice (stiff) pall as it was originally. The cut size of a corporal is
approximately twenty inches, depending on the depth of the altar.
Hems are usually at least a half inch with mitered corners. A corporal
may be embroidered with a symbol centered one to two inches
above the hem on one edge. It is traditionally folded in thirds, inside
out, so that only the wrong side of the cloth shows. When folded this
way, it can easily be unfolded into position right side up on the altar
and refolded from that position at the close of the Eucharist, encasing
whatever fragments may have fallen on it.

Purificator

A purificator is a square of medium weight fabric used to wipe and
dry the chalice during the Eucharist. A purificator may also be used
like a second corporal (instead of the stiff pall) or in any other way
the priest designates. A purificator is usually about twelve inches
square with hems as small as possible, but the size is really determined
by the size of the chalice with which it is to be used and over which it
may have to be draped. It is traditionally folded in thirds, right side
out, and its folded width should be slightly longer than the diameter
of the chalice cup. Purificators may be embroidered with a symbol in
the center, not necessarily in white.

Lavabo and Baptismal Towels

A towel is used during the Eucharist to dry the hands of the priest
after the ceremony of the lavabo or during baptism to dry the fore-
head of the baptized as well as the hands of the priest. Towels are
made of medium weight material cut twelve by eighteen inches or
any other convenient size. Hems are narrow, side hems narrower
than ends, and an embroidered white or colored symbol may be
centered an inch or so above the hem on one end. Although the
symbols may be keyed to the special use (a shell for baptism, a cross
for lavabo) the towels are interchangeable. They are traditionally
folded in thirds, lengthwise, then in half to hang easily over the
server's wrist.

Chalice Pall (Stiff Pall)

A chalice pall is a seven to nine inch plastic or cardboard square
covered tightly with medium to heavy weight material and embroidered simply or elaborately on one side. (If the square is cardboard,
the cover is made to be removable for washing.) The pall developed
from the original second corporal to which it is now giving place. In

the traditional manner of arranging the vessels for the Eucharist, the pall has been used to cover the paten holding the priest's wafer, thereby providing a firm base over which to drape the silk chalice veil. It has also been used during the Eucharist as a chalice cover to protect the wine from dust or insects. Because of today's departures from this tradition in the kinds of bread presented, the types of vessels used at the altar, and the manner of placing the vessels, a soft second corporal or large purificator, folded or unfolded, or an entirely new linen made to resemble these, is more satisfactory as a cover than the stiff pall. The bread is now often a loaf instead of wafers, the paten a bowl, a platter or a basket instead of a plate, and the vessels are often not nested or even placed on the altar until the offertory, when the Table is set. In these instances the purpose of a pall and a silk veil has disappeared and an altar guild can devise its own linens to cover the elements and the vessels in accordance with what the priest thinks is necessary.

Post-Communion Veil

A post-communion veil is a square of light weight fabric some-times used to drape the chalice and paten on the altar if they are not cleansed immediately after the communions of the people. This veil may also be used to cover consecrated elements that have been re-moved from the altar. Use of a post-communion veil is optional—a second corporal or a large purificator or another similar cloth will serve the same purpose. The size of the veil depends on the chalice it will cover, with allowance for hems and mitered corners. Embroidery is in the center and is often quite elaborate. The veil may be edged with lace or made entirely of lace pieces appliquéd to a suitable backing.

Aumbry or Tabernacle Veil

A aumbry veil is a curtain of fine material hung inside the door of the aumbry to veil the opening.

Credence and Other Table Covers

Small table covers are made of medium weight material cut to fit the tables and shelves they will cover, allowing for hems. They may be edged with lace or embroidered simply. (Elaborate embroidery may cause vessels to tip.)

DISPOSABLES

Disposable "linens" are particularly convenient for hospitals, conventions, summer camps, outdoor chapels and other places where it is not possible to care for linens properly after use. Disposables may also be convenient for home celebrations and other occasions when small groups or individuals receive the sacrament away from the church building or for any other celebrations when the priest chooses.

For years some priests have used plain white paper napkins, paper toweling or large-sized tissues for such occasions, sometimes folding the paper products to resemble the cloth articles. In order to standardize the use of such nonlinens and to ensure their dignified handling, the Presiding Bishop has approved the use of disposable purificators and towels (not corporals) for convenience and the method for making them devised by the National Association of Diocesan Altar Guilds.

This method stipulates that disposable purificators and towels be made from standard three-ply paper napkin stock in a size suitable for the purpose. (Three-ply napkins are stronger and more absorbent than two-ply and do not separate when ironed.) Napkins are refolded and pressed to resemble the cloth articles if desired, and stamped red with a crossed-crosslet stamp. Kits containing a stamp, a sample disposable purificator and full instructions for making one are available from the supply chairman of NADAG. Disposables are easily and quickly made and have been gratefully accepted by many clergy for use at special services.

CARE AND STORAGE OF LINENS

In keeping with their general philosophy about tending God's altar and caring for its appointments, altar workers handle church linens gently as they would any other delicate items. Careful laundering and repairing prolong life. All church linens therefore are usually washed by themselves in very hot water by hand or in a machine using the gentle cycle and rinsed until the water is clear of all soap or detergent. (Borax or washing soda will soften hard water and a cup of white vinegar in the final rinse will remove residual alkalis and soap particles.) As a rule they are not starched. Common stains can usually be removed by immediate treatment before washing, often simply by rubbing gently with mild detergent or soap. Appendix IV contains a list of suggestions for removing common "church stains."

Before trying commercial pre-wash products on a stain, it is important to know not only the qualities of the product, but the properties of the stain and of the material as well. Some products are too strong for the fabric or ineffectual for the stain. Using commercial bleaches containing chlorine is not advisable except as a last resort and then only with extreme care because chlorine tends to eat fine fabrics. If keeping chlorine bleach in the sacristy is unavoidable, reducing it to half strength and storing it in a small bottle will help to control its use and protect the fabrics on which it is used.

Although pure linen can be laundered easily and will last a long time, it does yellow with age and infrequent use. Articles should be rotated and laundered regularly to keep them fresh and white. Linen is not compatible with chemical bleaches or laundry detergents containing bleach, so restoring yellowed linen to whiteness is most easily achieved by the time-tested methods of sun bleaching or boiling gently for half an hour in water to which washing soda and a mild soap or detergent have been added.

Lace is durable if it is washed with a mild cold water wash product and ironed carefully while still damp. Lace may also be dried on a flat surface without ironing. The shape of the lace is stretched with the hands and the difficult points are carefully pinned down.

Ironing either pure or synthetic linens more than is necessary, especially ironing in folds, increases wear. If the sacristy has a formica countertop, freshly washed wet linens can be spread taut on the clean surface and smoothed firmly into shape to dry. They then can literally be peeled off the formica and finger-pressed for storage or put away flat and finger-pressed just before use. Any hard, glass-like surface, vertical or horizontal, can substitute for a formica counter.

Since few sacristies (or homes) have a large enough counter for the wet method to be used for a fair linen, it usually has to be ironed. A freshly washed fair linen refrigerated in a plastic bag for several hours can be ironed quite easily. A practical method is to iron the hems on the right side first; turn the linen and iron it completely on the wrong side; turn it again and iron it on the right side where needed (including the hems). Embroidery is usually ironed on the wrong side with a towel or absorbent padding under it. Hems and embroideries have to be thoroughly dry before rolling or folding.

Fair linens and credence or other table covers are better stored rolled than folded because folding inevitably makes creases which weaken the fabric. Rollers can be made from newspapers covered with plain paper or from cardboard tubes, like those from fabric or rug stores, cut to size. Covering the rollers with cloth (flannelette, for example) keeps the linens clean and prevents their slipping. If the linens are rolled right side down, the ends will curl toward the table when unrolled; if they are rolled right side up, they can be unrolled into position on the Table. A rolled linen stays fresh and clean when wrapped in tissue paper or placed in a plastic bag and stored in a drawer or on a shelf. (Acid-free tissue made especially for wrapping precious fabrics is available.)

If a fair linen cannot be rolled or hung for storage and has to be folded, padding the folds generously with tissue is important. Padding prevents the folds being fixed as creases. Folding the linen from both ends to the center several times, padding every fold, works well and reduces the linen to a size convenient for storing in a drawer or box. A linen so folded can be placed directly on the altar and unfolded into position.

A stitch in time is as important for church linens as it is for any other article. Most even-weave fabrics are easily darned, and small patches can be inconspicuous. Even chalice palls can have new corners appliquéd artistically. The emphasis in church linens is primarily on cleanliness and overall neatness. Since slightly noticeable repairs affect neither, they are usually acceptable to priests and are a good economic measure.

When linens have been replaced in one parish, they may still be useful in another. Frequently good storage space is given to linens which are no longer used but which are too good to throw away. Careful sacristy housekeeping involves finding new locations for old linens if possible (diocesan altar guilds can often help) or disposing of them with dignity by burning or burying.

Dressing Up

Vestments in General

For most of Christian history certain garments have been considered "traditional attire for the clergy." These garments share a double ancestry and reveal it even in their modern counterparts. Street clothing of the Graeco-Roman world, in which early Jewish-Christians lived, gave the men presiding at the first Christian ceremonies their dress: an outer cloak, an under tunic with a cord around the waist, a neckpiece, a scarf on the left wrist. This is what men and women of the upper classes ordinarily wore in the beginning of the Church. It may have been their best clothing, but it was nonetheless common to all. In those days of political and religious unrest, dressing like everyone else (if there was ever any idea of dressing otherwise) screened Christians from the eyes of would-be persecutors. As the Church grew in importance, respectability and size and moved out into the mission world of later centuries and other cultures, continuation of this early costume by conservative Christian leaders served to set them apart in the midst of the changing fashions of their times. Like a uniform, the costume designated their holy office and was considered "proper." When the functions of priesthood divided, leaders with different responsibilities dressed differently. The garments became more and more decorated with symbols and therefore became visual aids in the instruction of converts. Centuries later the early outfit was amplified by the customary black street habit of the monks of medieval universities such as the cassock, the overtunic (gown) with hood, the tippet and the cap.

These two lines of outerwear merged and have been adopted and adapted, added to and subtracted from, by clergy through subsequent centuries according to the customs and resources of their times and places. In the Middle Ages when knowledge of the historical origin of these garments had almost been forgotten, allegorical and symbolic meanings became associated with most of them, often inconsistent, sometimes inaccurate, always imaginative. During the years different materials, shapes, ornamentation, colors, even combinations of garments have been used, but the common lineage is obvious. The two lines have contributed to the contemporary formal dress of Christian clergy of all persuasions, if only in their "basic black." They are particularly recognizable in the attire of clergy in the one, holy, catholic and apostolic tradition, but even in this one tradition variation of all sorts has been rampant.

The Church of England tried at times, officially and unofficially, to introduce some degree of uniformity into vestment wear, with much discussion and little success. The Episcopal Church set the parameters for vestments and all other types of ceremonial at its beginning by stating in the Preface to the first *Book of Common Prayer* (1789):

> It is a most invaluable part of that blessed "liberty wherewith Christ hath made us free," that in his worship different forms and usages may without offence be allowed, provided the substance of the Faith be kept entire.

I tried only once to exercise some control of vestment wear in the 1870s, unsuccessfully.[16] The spirit of the Preface carried. Today canon law says nothing about vestment wear about type, material, design or occasion, and the rubrics in *The Book of Common Prayer* say very little.

On the other hand, in every period and every locale of the Church, concepts of beauty, new research and ideas of liturgical leaders, development of new materials, requirements of climate and economy, and not least, attitudes of local groups of worshipers, have had a great deal to say. The array of garments that has been created as a result has given priests of all orders a wide range from which to choose whatever dress they and their congregations can be comfortable with. The dress they choose is intended to enhance the worship and to give anonymity to the presiders by translating their personhood to priesthood. Color, material, design and ornamentation do this only when they do not draw the attention of the worshipers, priest and people alike, away from God.

Well-documented books about the history of vestments are available for people interested in tracing the particulars of change.[17] Some of them are fascinating. It is enough for most worshipers today to understand that change has been the rule, not the exception, and that it is still taking place for many valid reasons. There is no right or wrong in vesture. Choices and changes may be made, locally and regularly. An altar guild's responsibility is to learn how to care for, perhaps even how to make, the garments each of its successive priests chooses to wear, knowing that all priests have different ideas and that those ideas vary according to the occasion.

Choice lies first among the different types of vestments. Following that, a priest has to think about styles, materials, colors and ornamentation, as well as a number of practical matters like tradition and temperature, budget and architecture, in the parish church where the vestments will be worn. Weighing all these questions may not be new to priests, but finding them a normal part of vestment choice may be a new idea to people working with them, altar guilds in particular. It is important that vestments be in harmony with the decor of the building, pleasing to the eye and mind of the beholders, in keeping with the liturgical position of the parish, suitable for the period and the place where they will be worn, and becoming and comfortable for the priest who wears them.

All liturgical vestments can be worn by men and women alike but standard ready-made garments for priests are sized to men's dimensions and need considerable adjustment to fit women who are normally of smaller build. Ready-made stoles are too long for most women, for example, and chasubles too roomy. Some supply houses carry cassock-albs, cassocks, surplices, and shirts for street dress of standard design in standard women's sizes, but seldom the other vestments. An occasional vestment house specializes in attire for women, but frequently women are now making their own vestments or having them made to order. When they do so they can experiment with adapting suit, dress and jumper patterns to priestly lines for either liturgical or street use, emphasizing their womanhood in their dress as priests, instead of camouflaging it. With contemporary pattern-making aids and techniques, there is no limit to the possibilities for women's vestments.

As in the case of hangings, materials for vestments have always tended to be the best that people could afford among those suitable for the purpose. "Suitable" includes consideration of comfort and durability. The supposition that any one material could be proper or improper has no historical basis. In all times diversity has existed from parish to parish, even within one parish from generation to generation, so that silk and corduroy, linen and cotton, can often be found in one sacristy all made up into one type of vestment.

Whatever material makes up best into the garment, all things considered, is the "proper" material for that purpose. Twentieth century fabrics differ from those developed in earlier centuries, as do twentieth century expressions of art, and they have their own beauty. In sacristies today, side by side with elegant vestments created from damask and tapestry, wool and linen, appliquéd or embroidered with classic symbols, hang comparably beautiful vestments created from wrinkle-free, easy-care, durable, lightweight, washable "miracle" fabrics in a wide range of colors, appliquéd or embroidered in contemporary designs.

Colors from the entire spectrum appear in vestments as well as hangings today, just as they did in vestments of the late Middle Ages. Until that time color was not a critical matter. In fact for years white vestments for clergy had been preferred. Once colors were introduced in the Church, the emphasis seems to have been on beautifying the service of worship in the loveliest ways possible, following no particular color system, even using many colors at once. Restrictions had to do with reserving the best for the greatest feasts, whatever the color. In some churches red was the prevailing color year round. At a later period associations grew between colors and moods, and eventually between colors and the times of the Church year. White and gold were associated with purity and joy, green and yellow with growth; purple with dignity; red with leadership and martyrdom; dark blue, violet and black with sadness. More or less set patterns of color use developed in one part of the church or another, and finally in the late sixteenth century, Rome pulled these various patterns together rubrically into a standard sequence geared symbolically to the Church seasons and holy days. There was some latitude in this sequence (different shades, alternate colors), but the familiar white, green, red, violet and black of Western church calendars evolved from it.

The Church of England followed this color sequence in its early years, but generally ignored it after the Reformation. Between 1600 and 1900 the Anglican communion was basically black and white in dress on both sides of the Atlantic. Late in the nineteenth century a move back to Eucharistic vestments and the five colors began and has been progressing steadily ever since. Church calendars dated in color and commercial vestment houses have influenced the move, but as Church calendars are not binding on the Church nor commercial houses official in any way, colored vestments are still not worn in all parishes, even in this last quarter of the twentieth century.

Some priests continue to dress in black and white, though usually with a colored stole. At the same time, however, other priests are bringing a wide variety of colors into the Church—not only the alternate colors of the Roman sequence, but all shades and colors of the spectrum. The vesting of clergy has a whole new dimension.

Vestments in Particular

Priestly garments are usually classified for conversational reference. Traditionally the term Eucharistic vestments has included chasuble, maniple, stole, girdle, alb and amice (together with dalmatic and tunicle). Choir dress has been cassock and surplice with tippet (scarf) and the optional academic hood. The Bishop's vestments include rochet, chimere and scarf, and the bishop's emblems of office are ring, crozier (staff) and mitre. Other apparel not falling into these three groups includes cassock (the basic undergarment), cope, cloak, caps and clerical street dress. Good illustrations of the current styles of most of these vestments can be found in church vestment catalogues. Descriptions of the vestments, their origin, their use and their contemporary counterparts follow this section.

Vestment classification is convenient, but today the traditional terms are sometimes confusing because they don't always apply. Of course no one wears the Bishop's vestments except a bishop, but other usage is more flexible than is implied by the terms. The Eucharistic vestments above, for example, (except the stole) are worn only for presiding at the Eucharist, but all six are no longer always worn, nor is it required that they be worn at all. It is just as permissible today for a priest or a bishop to preside at the Holy Table in street dress as it was in the early years of the Church and in informal situations they often do. It is also not unusual for a priest to preside at the Eucharist in surplice and stole (over a cassock) or a bishop in rochet, chimere and scarf as they have done in the Episcopal Church for most of its history. Other vestments suitable for the Eucharist are cassock-alb and stole, with or without girdle or chasuble; chasuble-alb and stole; or cope and stole.

The only rubrics pertaining to vestments in *The Book of Common Prayer* are in the "Episcopal Services" section, primarily in the ordination rites. The candidates are to be presented: the bishop-elect in "rochet or alb, without stole, tippet, or other vesture distinctive of ecclesiastical or academic rank or order" (p. 511); the ordinands to the priesthood and diaconate "in surplice or alb, without stole, tippet . . . " (pp. 524, 536). After the prayer of consecration the new bishop is "vested according to the order of bishops" (p. 521) i.e. chimere (the exclusively episcopal vestment) and scarf with the rochet; or chasuble, stole and mitre (or cope, stole and mitre) with the alb. Later the new bishop may be given "other symbols of office" (p. 521) i.e. "a ring, staff, and mitre, or other suitable insignia of office" (p. 553). The new priest, after the prayer of consecration, is "vested according to the order of priests" (p. 534) with "the stole worn about the neck or other insignia of the office of priest" (p. 553) and the new deacon "according to the order of deacons" (p. 545) with "the stole worn over the left shoulder, or other insignia of the office of deacon" (p. 554). The new minister, in the rite for Celebrating a New Ministry, is presented with "a stole or other symbol" (p. 561), and the bishop at the Dedication of a Church marks the threshold "with the pastoral staff (or the foot of the processional cross)" when the door is open (p. 568).

No other clerical vesture is mentioned in the Prayer Book. No other rubrics and no canon laws specify garments for different functions. Except for the stole, the emblem of ordination, the vesture clergy choose to wear on different occasions is a matter of taste and judgment, tempered by local custom. With both "traditional" vestments and new vestments to choose among, and a number of combinations possible for everyone, classification in a manner slightly different from the familiar one described above may be useful to altar guilds and clergy alike. Vestments for all ministers, lay and ordained, can be categorized as undergarments and outergarments for the Eucharist and for choir dress and the other sacraments. Emblems of office for bishops, priests and deacons would be a separate category, as would "other vestments"—outdoor clothing, for example.

The basic undergarment for choir dress is the cassock in one of its various forms topped by a surplice for lay assistants, by surplice and tippet (with a hood if desired) for priests and deacons, and by rochet, chimere, and scarf (with a hood if desired) for bishops. (The cassock is often omitted under the rochet.) A plain cassock-alb girded or ungirded or a chasuble-alb is suitable for anyone to wear for choir dress, with or without a cassock.

The basic undergarment for Eucharistic dress is the alb (with amice) or its modern variants the cassock-alb or the chasuble-alb. The chasuble-alb is worn with or without a cassock, ungirded (plain for lay assistants), topped by a stole for clergy. The alb (with amice) is worn with or without a cassock, usually girded (lay assistants), topped by a stole and a chasuble (bishop or priest), a dalmatic (deacon), or a cope (bishop). A maniple is optional. The cassock-alb may be worn in the manner of either the chasuble-alb or the traditional alb. The bishop's choir dress minus the hood is entirely suitable for presiding at the Eucharist as is the priest's if a stole takes the place of the tippet and hood.

The insignia of ordination for priests and deacons are stole and maniple (though the latter is seldom used today). Episcopal insignia are mitre, staff and ring.

A note here about vesting for concelebration. The rubric (pp. 322, 354), "It is appropriate that the other priests present stand with the celebrant at the Altar" allows any priests present in the church to concelebrate, vested similarly or not. To limit concelebration to those who can vest for the occasion according to a rule seems to restrict the intent of the rubric. However, when it is possible to plan ahead for concelebration, all participants may vest exactly alike, or the principal celebrant may vest in chasuble or cope and stole and the others alike in surplice or alb or cassock-alb and stole, or all may vest in chasubles matched in color but designed to distinguish the principal celebrant from the others.

Cassocks

Whether or not cassocks are considered to be "vestments" in the strict sense, they certainly vest all who participate in leading services in the Church—clergy, crucifers, acolytes, servers, layreaders, choir. A cassock is the traditional floor length basic tunic which may be worn alone or under other vestments.

Clergy cassocks are commonly black, but those for lay assistants may be in any appropriate color. Cassocks for the bishop and the whole cathedral staff have traditionally been purple. Sometimes the purple has been limited to purple piping and buttons on black. Sometimes the tone of purple has seemed important—blue-purple in the cathedral, red-purple outside. The material and style of cassocks depends on preference.

Cassocks come in three styles, all full-length, close-fitting, long-sleeved, and high-necked, with a front-opening mandarin neckline designed to wear over the back-fastening "clerical" collar. The Latin (Roman) style buttons or zips center front, neck to hem. The Anglican style overlaps fully in front, the opening on the right side front fastened with snaps, buttons or velcro at both shoulders and waist. The Jesuit style partially overlaps in front, fastening at center waist and neck. All three styles may be belted with a matching rope or sash cincture/girdle or a leather belt. (The Anglican style is usually belted with a sash.)

CASSOCK
Anglican

CASSOCK
Roman

The cassock is a descendent of the Roman citizen's black tunic which clergy were required to wear in the sixth century. In one form or another cassocks have been part of clergy dress ever since. In many countries for many years (including England until the nineteenth century) cassocks were normal street attire for clergy and only recently have they ceased being the undergarment for all other vestments.

Alb

An alb is a long, white, straight-cut, collarless tunic with long close-fitting sleeves and short buttoned front neck opening. It reaches to the feet in order to completely cover a cassock if one is worn under it. The alb is descended from the white Roman under tunic, the *tunica alba*, the traditional undergarment of all Christians in the early centuries. The alb was worn by all clergy for all services until the eleventh century when the surplice began to replace it for non-Eucharistic services.

Albs have had times of elegance (embroidery, lace, colored silk) and times of simplicity (plain white linen or wool). Modern albs are plain and made of any durable white material, usually "easy-care." The custom of sometimes decorating them at front and back hems and cuffs with "apparels" (oblong colored bands, normally detachable) goes back to the eleventh century. (If the alb is apparelled, the amice usually is also.)

Amice

The word *amicio* means to wrap around. An amice is a rectangle of white cloth with long string ties which is wrapped around the neck like a kerchief to give a collar effect and protect the other more ornate vestments. Amices are sometimes made with attached embroidered collars in self-material or with apparels.

The custom of wearing an amice as a liturgical vestment began about the eighth century, but with the advent of cassock-albs and chasuble-albs which have collars, amices are falling into disuse. When one is worn, it is donned before the alb, the square of material being placed across the shoulders and the ties secured around the body; it is adjusted to collar position when the alb is on. The sometime custom of first placing it on the head like a hood, then settling it to collar position after donning the other vestments, originated in the tenth century probably to keep from disarranging the long hair styles of the day.

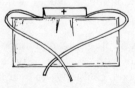

ALB

AMICE

GIRDLE

Girdle / Cincture

Today these terms have become interchangeable for the long cord and the wide band (sash) used to belt an alb or a cassock. The color matches the garment. First century Roman dress included a cord girding the under tunic. In early church terminology a girdle was the cord and a cincture the band, and most old altar guild manuals indicate this distinction.

The band fastens snugly about the waist and is usually made with sash ends. The cord is worn doubled with either alb or cassock, and is long enough for the ends to hang below the knee. An alb is usually girded with the cord, an Anglican cassock with the band. Use of either with the other cassocks or the cassock-alb is a matter of preference. A leather belt is occasionally used with black cassocks.

Cassock-Alb

The modern cassock-alb is white or off-white, made in a variety of materials. It incorporates the cassock shape with the alb/surplice white and the amice neckband (in a stand up collar or a soft hood). It may be belted with a rope or sash girdle. It does not need a cassock under it.

For the sacraments, priests wear a cassock-alb with a stole hanging either straight or crossed, deacons with it over the left shoulder. Addition of a chasuble or dalmatic or tunicle for presiding or assisting at the Eucharist is optional. A plain cassock-alb is suitable choir dress. In increasing numbers lay assistants in services wear cassock-albs, white in the sanctuary, white or colored in the choir.

Surplice

A surplice is related to the alb, much fuller and somewhat shorter, made with a yoke and wide sleeves. Surplices first appeared in the eleventh century to go over the fur-lined cassocks which were worn in cold churches. (The word surplice comes from *superpelliceum* meaning "over fur.") Through the years surplices have varied in cut from very full and ankle-length to straight and knee-length. They have had round and square yokes, sleeves of different shapes, have been made of various white materials, and have been both plain and decorated. The full version is quite similar in shape to albs and dalmatics pictured in early mosaics.

CASSOCK-ALB   SURPLICE

Today surplices are generally made from any easy-care white material which will drape and launder well, and they are cut very full. They usually hang from a round yoke, extend to several inches below the knee, and are sometimes embroidered with an emblem center front. The surplice is white; all other stylistic details are a matter of preference.

From the time of Elizabeth I to the late nineteenth century "surplice and cassock" (without stole or tippet) was normal priestly garb for all services in the Church of England,[18] and also in the Episcopal Church as vesture became acceptable. Today, with tippet and hood, it is one option for choir dress, and with stole it is an option for the Eucharist and the other sacraments. Lay assistants in worship often wear surplice and cassock.

Cotta

A cotta is an abbreviated version of a surplice—shorter body, shorter round sleeves, round or square yoke. Cottas may be worn by acolytes, servers and choir, but are not customarily worn by other lay assistants or by clergy in the Church of England or the Episcopal Church.

Tippet and Hood

Originally the black tippet (scarf) was probably part of the hood worn in the Middle Ages with a black gown as everyday clothing in the universities. Eventually the hood was separated and "tippet and hood" became part of clergy choir dress in the Church of England and the Episcopal Church. Neither is worn for the Eucharist because both represent personal (academic) achievement.

A hood is worn around the neck hanging down the back. Its length denotes the academic degree, the colored silk lining denotes the university or seminary, the colored velvet banding denotes the field of study. A tippet is worn around the neck scarf-like, lying over the hood at the shoulders. It is wide, today usually pleated at the neck for fit, and frequently decorated on the ends with emblems of church or school. A tippet may be worn without a hood. (A bishop's scarf is related to a tippet.)

STOLE   TIPPET

Stole

A stole is a long narrow neck scarf worn by ordained clergy when presiding or assisting at the Eucharist and the other sacraments. It is the emblem of their ordination. A deacon wears a stole over the left shoulder, the ends either hanging straight front and back or crossing the body to be secured in some way under the right arm. A priest wears a stole around the neck, the ends either hanging straight in front or crossing on the breast to be held in place by the girdle. A bishop wears a stole around the neck with the ends hanging straight in front.

A stole may be worn either over or under the chasuble or the dalmatic, or over the surplice, the cassock-alb, or the chasuble-alb. Today's "pallium stole," a circle of material with wide strips hanging front and back, is a version of the early pallium—a white wool scarf reserved for bishops and archbishops, worn loosely about the neck, the ends crossed on the left shoulder and hanging back and front.

This pallium for a bishop, together with an orarium for a priest, was the first version of the stole as a liturgical vestment. The custom of wearing these scarves spread gradually, ordered by councils and ritual books in different parts of the Church in the West from the seventh century on. By the twelfth century the name stole had long since been given to both, and stoles were in general use as the priestly mark of office. In the Church of England from the time of Elizabeth I until late in the nineteenth century the stole fell into disuse, but since then both there and in the Episcopal Church stoles are once again the emblem of ordination.

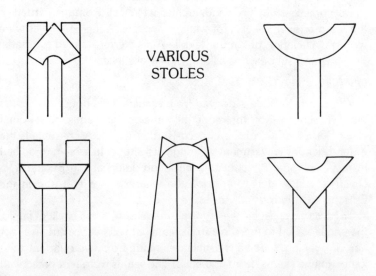

VARIOUS
STOLES

Stoles have varied in length and shape from very long to very short, from narrow to wide to contoured. They have been white or colored; linen, silk, or other materials; plain or elaborate with embroidery and fringe. Before the Reformation it was usual for stole and maniple to match, contrasting with the other vestments. Today's stoles appear in many materials and in all colors. They do not necessarily match any other vestments and often are neutral so they will blend with all. Some are hand woven. Some are decorated with classic or contemporary designs embroidered or appliquéd simply or elaborately on the ends or along the entire length, and some are undecorated. Stoles still vary in length and shape and some contemporary forms are quite stylized, but generally speaking they

are long enough and wide enough to make a clear statement of what
they are—the sign of priesthood.

Maniple

A maniple is a short narrow wrist scarf matching the stole in color
and material which, in some form, clergy have worn for the Eucharist
since the early years of the Church. Today maniples are falling into
disuse in the Anglican and Roman communions.

The maniple of earliest Eucharistic dress was related to the *mappa*
of the Roman consul, a folded linen napkin which he carried in his
hand as an ornament of his rank and waved or thrown down as a
signal for games to start. This mappa was in turn derived from a
purely practical napkin/handkerchief which all Romans carried in
the hand or over the arm for want of pockets. At first maniples were
worn by all clerics, but in the Middle Ages were restricted to priests,
deacons and subdeacons as an insignia of office.

Chasuble

The word chasuble is derived from *casula*, "little house" or tent, a
word descriptive of the early all-enveloping, semicircular outer
cloak, the *paenula*, of the Graeco-Roman world. A chasuble is the
outer Eucharistic vestment. Though its shape has been modified
from the original for convenience in presiding at the Eucharist, a
chasuble is intended to envelop the wearer like a tent and in the
Episcopal Church usually does.

The historic chasuble was conical, made from a half circle of fabric,
the edges folded to meet in a front seam with allowance cut away for
a neck opening. Often a chasuble was made from two quarter circles
joined in two seams, front and back. The seams were reinforced with
appliquéd bands which remained as purely decorative front and back
stripes (orphreys—gold work) when the garment was rotated to
place the seams at the sides. As clergy rose in importance in society,
their chasubles grew in elegance, coming to resemble royal garments
in color, material and decoration. Tapestry, brocade, velvet and
cloth of silver or gold as well as ornamentation in intricate designs
and often jewels made them robes of great beauty. Orphreys around
neck and edges were added, including two to make a cross of the
back band.

During the years the shape of the chasuble has gone through
dozens of adaptations, some for practical reasons, but today's
chasubles are closer in shape to the early tent-like ones than the

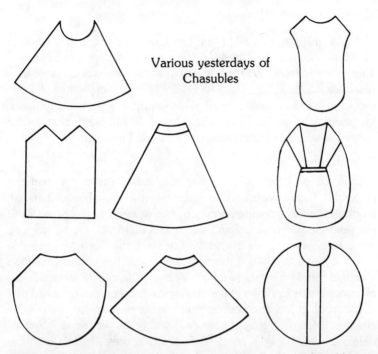

Various yesterdays of
Chasubles

majority of the intervening designs have been. Today's chasubles are
made of many materials besides traditional silks and wools, most of
them practical in terms of care and climate. Chasubles may be in any
color at all, multi-colored or neutral. They may be plain or decorated
with modern designs or traditional symbols. Orphreys may be used
in old or new arrangements or omitted entirely. Good taste and the
priest's wishes are the only restrictions to imagination in creating
modern chasubles.

CHASUBLE

Chasuble-Alb

A chasuble-alb is an all-in-one Eucharistic vestment. It is white or off-white, sleeved, and hooded for a composite cassock-alb-amice effect, but full and seamed in the front with a neck opening to resemble the chasuble as well. A chasuble-alb is worn with a stole on top so is usually not decorated. This vestment is particularly useful for priests who travel between parishes or live in warm climates for concelebrants, and for presiders at informal Eucharists.

Dalmatic and Tunicle

Dalmatic and tunicle are lesser Eucharistic vestments than the chasuble. Today each usually resembles the chasuble in material, length, fullness and ornamentation, but squared at the hem, slit at the sides below the waist, and sleeved. A dalmatic may be worn by the person serving as deacon at the Eucharist, the Gospeler according to rubric (pp.322, 354). A tunicle is shorter and less ornamented than a dalmatic and often has narrower sleeves. The tunicle was traditionally worn by the Epistoler at the Eucharist whether lay or ordained (the subdeacon). It has also been worn by lesser participants such as the crucifer. Maniples may be worn with both vestments. Neither dalmatic nor tunicle is required Eucharistic dress. In fact with the emphasis of the *Book of Common Prayer* on lay participation in the liturgy, epistolers are frequently unvested members of the congregation and deacons tend to vest simply in surplice or cassock-alb and stole. However, both vestments are historical church attire and can be worn if desired.

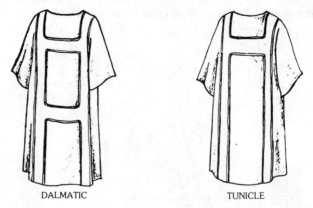

DALMATIC   TUNICLE

Like other vestments, dalmatic and tunicle originated in Roman street dress. The earliest dalmatics were a variant of the alb, wide sleeved over-tunics worn over the alb for a second layer of clothing. In frescoes they resemble the later, very full, long, wide-sleeved medieval surplice. Later dalmatics were shortened, the sides slit, and the sleeves reshaped and they were made of richer materials and ornamented. Tunicles followed suit but were less festive than dalmatics. Although these vestments were for deacons and sub-deacons, it was not unusual for higher ranking clergy to wear both tunicle and dalmatic over the alb and under the chasuble.

Bishop's Vestments: Rochet, Chimere and Scarf

A rochet is a derivative of the alb. It is an enveloping white vest-ment worn under a chimere, ungirded and with or without a cassock. One form is quite similar to the alb—not too full with straight sleeves. The more usual rochet is ample in body like a surplice but it hangs to the feet. The sleeves are large and full length, gathered and secured at the wrist with either stiff fluted cuffs and a narrow red or black ribbon band or narrow straight cuffs and a wider red or black band. (The ribbon matches the chimere.) The cuffs are usually detachable to simplify laundering. The material for the rochet has traditionally been lawn or fine linen, but any good quality white material is suit-able, preferably an easy-care variety.

The rochet was at first worn generally by clergy and by lay people assisting at the liturgy. Toward the end of the Middle Ages it became reserved for bishops and some other dignitaries. At that time it was narrow-sleeved or sleeveless. The huge sleeves developed in the

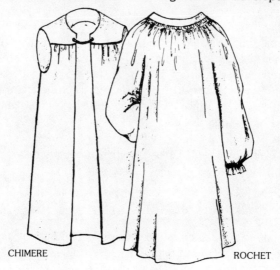

CHIMERE   ROCHET

Church of England after "rochet and chimere" were prescribed as episcopal dress in the time of Elizabeth I. At one period the sleeves worn by Anglican bishops were so full that they were attached to the chimere instead of the rochet.

The chimere is a black or scarlet academic gown like that for a doctor, only sleeveless. Although traditionally silk or satin, a chimere may be made of any substantial material according to preference. It is worn over a rochet and topped by a scarf, a bishop's long version of a tippet. "Rochet and chimere" appeared in the Church in the Middle Ages and (as noted above) became liturgical and civil dress for bishops in England in the sixteenth century.

A bishop may preside at the Eucharist in either rochet, chimere and scarf, or alb, chasuble (or cope) and stole with mitre if desired. Normally garments in these sets of vestments are not exchanged. A new bishop at ordination is vested to preside at the ordination Eucharist. The garments added at that time depend on the basic garment the new bishop is wearing. A Church of England tradition has the bishop vested in stole, cope and mitre for the Eucharist, because there the cope is the bishop's Eucharistic vestment.

Bishop's Emblems of Office

A ring has been given to a new bishop at consecration as an emblem of office since the seventh century. The ring is a signet ring bearing the bishop's personal seal. It is often set with an amethyst, traditional color of the episcopate, and is worn on the third finger of the right hand.

Originally the (pastoral) staff was just a staff, a walking stick. The crook shape and the accompanying symbolism related to shepherds came in the Middle Ages as did the name crozier, from a medieval French/Latin word meaning bearer of the crook. In the seventh century staffs were given to new bishops at consecration in some places as a sign of office, and by the end of the eighth were recognized all through the West.

A crozier is made of wood or various metals, sometimes precious. It may be plain or jeweled. Today's croziers are made to be collapsed for easy packing.

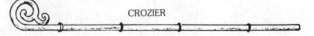

CROZIER

The bishop carries the crozier in procession and during ceremonial occasions in the left hand with the crook top facing toward the "flock." Because the crozier is a sign of office not of jurisdiction, it is not customary for the Bishop's chaplain to hold the crozier unless the bishop's hands are not free as during confirmation. Although the Presiding Bishop and archbishops may carry croziers because of their order as bishops, they also have primatial crosses or cross-staffs because of their jurisdiction. A primatial cross is a staff topped with a small cross. It is properly carried like a banner before the Presiding Bishop or archbishop in procession.

According to Cyril Pocknee: "There is no ancient or proper authority which suggests that a bishop may not carry his crozier outside his diocese, or that suffragan bishops may not carry their pastoral staffs in the presence of Archbishops and Diocesan Bishops. The crozier is the emblem of episcopal rank and not one of mere jurisdiction."[19]

A mitre is a bishop's "crown" first used by some Christian bishops through Papal grants in the eleventh century. By the end of the twelfth century so many bishops had received these grants that the mitre became an accepted part of the bishop's costume everywhere. This is an interesting development, since all earlier Christian wear of mitre-like headgear had apparently been reserved to deaconesses and abbesses. The first mitres were made conical. The cone was later rounded, then dented in the middle, like the top of a heart. In this shape it was rotated forty-five degrees and the rounded ends were pointed forming the basic double-pointed headgear for bishops that is familiar today. Two lappets, vestigial ties, hang in the back.

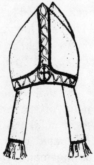

MITRE

The word mitre comes from a Latin word meaning turban, descriptive of the mitre's close fit. Mitres have been both plain and elaborate, linen and silk, even gold and silver, short and tall, according to preference. Mitres were out of use in England for some time, because of the Reformation aversion to ceremony and because of the custom of wearing wigs. When Bishop Seabury, the first American Episcopal Bishop, ordered a mitre from England in 1786, English vestment makers, having no current models to copy and no patterns to follow, had to resort to pictures to work out a design.[20]

A bishop may wear a mitre at confirmations and ordinations, in processions, and during parts of the Eucharist. The mitre is worn with either a cope or a chasuble but it does not have to match either one. In fact, it is often deliberately unmatched so that it may be worn with any cope or chasuble.

Although it is now customary for Anglican bishops to wear pectoral crosses, the custom is young (nineteenth century). The cross is not an emblem of office; it is only an ornament for the bishop, to be worn on a cord or a chain around the neck. Pectoral crosses vary from very plain to very ornate and may be given to new bishops as gifts at consecration.

Other Vestments

Cope

The cope is not exclusively an episcopal vestment but it has normally been such a costly garment that in many dioceses only a cathedral could afford one. Copes, therefore, became popularly associated with bishops who wear "cope and mitre" in processions and sometimes during the episcopal services at the cathedral and elsewhere. A cope, however, may be worn by any participant in any service. It has commonly been reserved for great processions and important occasions like weddings and funerals because of its elegance.

A traditional cope is an ornate cloak, an outdoor garment adapted for ceremonial use. It is actually an open-front conical chasuble in cut, fastened on the breast with a large and often jeweled velvet or metal clasp called a morse. It has a real or simulated hood. Copes have customarily been made of rich material in brilliant colors (tapestry, silk, velvet, cloth of gold) but need not be. They have usually been elaborately decorated with orphreys, tassels, fringe, braid or jewels in various arrangements, particularly a wide orphrey around the neck and down both sides of the front. Modern copes are also elegant, but the elegance is generally in material and cut more than in ornamentation.

Like the chasuble, the cope traces its ancestry to Roman days, to the paenula of the soldier. It is easily recognizable in the sixth century

COPE

mosaics of Ravenna, so was obviously worn in some parts of the early Church, but it was not in general church use until the tenth and eleventh centuries. It has been an alternate Eucharistic vestment since the Reformation, but was not common in the Episcopal Church until the twentieth century.

Cloak

A clerical cloak is a warm, roomy, useful outdoor garment, full length and traditionally black. It is semicircular, has pockets and a collar, and fastens with a button or hook at the neck and a frog at the breast. Cloaks are of different weight (and warmth) and may have detachable hoods. A *cappa nigra* is also an outdoor garment, fuller than the cloak but similar, with a functional attached hood. It is in effect a black wool cope.

Hats

A biretta is a squared cap of stiffened black material with three blades and a pompon on top. The bladeless corner goes to the left. A person with a doctorate is entitled to a fourth blade. A biretta may be worn in church services or out of doors. (A bishop's biretta is purple with a green lining, or red, or black with purple piping and pompon.)

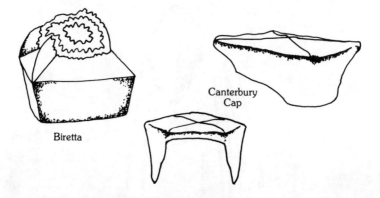

Biretta

Canterbury
Cap

A square or canterbury cap is an adaptation of the academic mortar-board for outdoor wear. It is black with soft sides fitting close around the back of the head and ears and the loosely encased "board" framing the face.

The shovel hat is also black and worn outdoors. It is shallow-crowned with a wide brim curving upward all around.

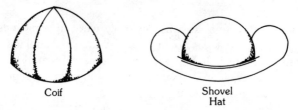

Coif

Shovel
Hat

Zuchetto and coif are two names for the skullcap (black for a priest, red or purple for a bishop) sometimes worn in the church during service.

The Silk Burse and Chalice Veil

In old altar guild manuals the burse and chalice veil are frequently listed with vestments although they vest the chalice, not the clergy. For many years they have been a familiar sight vesting the chalice on the altar before and after the service, but today's increasing practice of keeping the altar bare (or at most covered only by the cloths) until the offertory and clearing it entirely after the communion has removed the need for them. There is no chalice on the altar to vest. The burse may still be useful as a carrying case for small linens and the veils may find a new purpose as small funeral palls for urns of ashes, but their original use is fast departing.

The burse or corporas case as it was once called is a large cloth-covered, stiffened envelope, eight or ten inches square, plain or decorated. It may match the altar hangings and/or priest's vestments, but it has not always done so nor does it have to. The burse was designed originally to carry the two corporals to the Table—one to go under the chalice and one to go over it (which later developed into the stiff pall.) Extra purificators have since been added to the contents for the priest's convenience.

Although the burse is an ancient vestment, the silk veil arrived late in the Church of England from Rome and stirred much controversy about its validity as a vestment.[21] The veil is a square of silk or other material, usually but not always matching the burse in design and color. It is often lined for reinforcement so that it will drape well. When the veil is used, it covers the chalice and paten on the altar before and after the Great Thanksgiving, with the burse on top. It is large enough to hang to the Table on all four sides.

Verger's Gown

The traditional verger's gown resembles an academic gown, but the sleeves are distinctive. They hang straight like wide double scarves with pointed ends, the top layer shorter than the bottom, the opening for the arm between the two. It is usually made in a substantial black material and is sometimes trimmed in velvet. Today vergers often wear standard academic gowns, perhaps with velvet bands. The verger carries a wand-like mace or verge in procession, the emblem of his position as the official who "makes way for" (hence, leads) the procession.

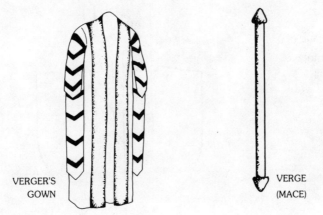

VERGER'S
GOWN

VERGE
(MACE)

"Clericals"

Street dress of the clergy is not the responsibility of an altar guild but familiarity with the names and styles of the different items of clerical street dress may be useful and can be gained from any church vestment catalogue.

Preparation and Care of Vestments

Preparation

To prepare the vestments for a service other than the Eucharist (cassock and surplice or cassock-alb and girdle), altar workers can leave them on their hangers in a place where they will be convenient for the priest when vesting—with the stole or tippet-and-hood near at hand. (The hood is optional.) The same preparation applies if the priest wears "surplice and stole" (or cassock-alb and stole) for the Eucharist.

In a parish where the priest wears the traditional complement of Eucharistic vestments (amice, alb, girdle, stole, maniple and chasuble), the altar guild will find the pattern for laying out the vestments in the order of donning them (as diagrammed in old manuals and wall charts) practical, if space allows.

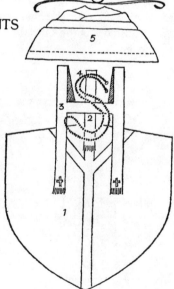

EUCHARIST VESTMENTS

1. Chasuble
2. Maniple
3. Stole
4. Girdle
5. Alb
6. Amice

Some priests continue the custom of saying, as they put on each garment, the old Latin vesting prayers prescribed by the Council of Trent in 1570 (see Appendix VI). These prayers have also been part of the background of some altar guild members, as have the allegorical meanings some vestments acquired from one source or another during the Middle Ages and the symbolism that gradually became attached to the functional method of "laying out." All these traditions have complicated the process of change for altar guilds.

And there is change. Most priests in the Church today are not following tradition in their choice of vestments. The cassock-alb is generally supplanting the cassock-alb-amice combination; the girdle is usually not needed if the stole is worn over the chasuble instead of under it; and the maniple is infrequently worn today by the celebrant. The surviving vestments to be "laid out" may be simply the stole and chasuble (in that order if the stole is worn on top). If the all-inclusive chasuble-alb is worn, only the stole remains. Cassock-albs and chasuble-albs are more easily donned (and stay neater) if left on hangers in a place convenient for the priest.

The altar guild's task in any setting—parish church, chapel, cathedral, conference center, field or home—is to devise a workable plan for having the vestments ready before any service. There is no rule to follow except convenience. The priest-in-charge chooses what he will wear and what any assistants in the sanctuary will wear for each occasion. The altar guild's responsibility for the vestments of people in the sanctuary besides the celebrant varies: sometimes these people are part of the church staff whose vestments are kept in the sacristy and need to be cared for and made ready at service time; sometimes the people are visitors who bring their own garments although extras for emergencies are a good idea. With the variety of services *The Book of Common Prayer* provides, most of them in the context of the Eucharist, and the possible number of people at the altar (celebrant, concelebrants, deacons, lay chalice bearers), the altar guild's "workable plan for having the vestments ready before any service" sometimes requires a great deal of ingenuity as well as common sense. Part of the freedom to worship is the freedom to work out the plans for it.

Care

Care of vestments requires local solutions. They have to be kept clean and neat and in good condition like any other clothes in which people dress up for special occasions. A stitch in time, immediate

spot removal, frequent touch-ups with an iron, and careful storage—
all these prolong life.

Laundering, dry cleaning and repairing depend on materials,
ornamentation, history, age and value of the vestments, as well as
the time and skill and number of altar guild workers. Polyester is one
thing, brocade another, and common housekeeping sense prevails.
Some vestments can be washed out and hung to drip-dry in some
sacristies, but most need to go to more spacious home laundries or
commercial cleaners known for good work with fine garments. Major
mending tasks need expert hands just as major cleaning tasks do. If
mending projects are beyond the skill of local needleworkers, inquiry
among convents, historical societies, textile museums[22] or diocesan
altar guilds may produce the help needed not too far afield.

"Accessory items" can be kept in drawers and cupboards but most
other vestments last longer if kept on padded hangers, preferably in
separate garment bags. Some sacristies have built-in banks of racks
over which chasubles hang; others have large shallow drawers in
which chasubles can be laid flat or almost flat, with tissue cushioning
folds and embroidery; still others have ample closets.

Many sacristies are at the other extreme and since careful storage
is essential to the life of vestments, altar guilds in such places have to
improvise. Closets, fixed or movable, elsewhere in the building will
serve this purpose. In old churches, closets and chests were often
incorporated into the decor of the nave, handsome wood carving
outside masking storage space within. Sometimes the altar was
moved out from the east end of the church and a wall was built
across the chancel behind it. This wall screened a space used not
only for storing vestments and hangings but for vesting as well. Both
these storage ideas have been copied in some modern churches.

Vestments more than most other furnishings tend to multiply, new
ones of all types being added from time to time to replace worn ones
or to introduce new materials, new designs, new colors or new sizes.
The space the supplanted ones take up could be put to better use, as
could those vestments themselves. Someone always has a use for
replaced vestments. Even still good ornamentation of badly worn
vestments can be used in refurbishing others. Most diocesan altar
guilds can help parish guilds to find places for these garments in other
parts of the Church family.

Part of the care of vestments is awareness of their value in case
emergency forces replacement. An item by item regularly updated
descriptive inventory and appraisal filed off the church premises for

safety is important. Ownership should always be indicated as some vestments kept in the sacristy may be the personal property of the priest.

Making Vestments

For people interested in making vestments, the first step is consultation with the priest. The priest is the final authority on what is appropriate and what will be used. With the priest's blessing, however, and his or her approval of intended design, style and material, people who are interested can make a significant offering of time and talent through vestment creation.

Kits of precut material available from some church supply houses are perhaps a good place for beginners to start because the expert cutting and careful instructions will lead to a presentable first product and add a feeling of confidence to a beginning effort. Men and women who are more adventuresome and want to create garments "from whole cloth" will discover many excellent books of instruction about ecclesiastical needlework of all kinds in book stores and libraries. Appendix V contains an annotated list of some of these. Regional chapters of the Embroiderers Guild of America usually have classes and workshops open to anyone interested in learning about embroidery and some diocesan altar guilds provide instruction in the basics of vestment making.

The people of God have different gifts to offer, different talents to put to work. Stitchery is one of these. The diversity of materials, colors and designs coming into use in the Church today beckons those whose love for God can be expressed with a needle, and the Church is ready for them liturgically. Today's understanding of the "work of the people" in worship involves far more than taking part in worship services.

Other Occasions

Altar guild manuals have in the past devoted a considerable amount of space to instructing parish altar guilds in preparation for the seasons of the Church year, the holy days and the important times of a Christian's life. There has been no attempt to do so in this book because parishes observe these times of the Church in quite individual ways. They develop parish rites and ceremonies for these special times within the context of the rubrics of the Prayer Book, just as individual families develop home rites and ceremonies for their special occasions within the context of a social custom. Birthdays at home, for example, are filled with anticipated family words and actions (cards, greetings, traditional meals or decorations) as well as the birthday cake and song of social custom. Christmas at church, for example, is filled with anticipated parish words and actions (a pageant, "traditional" decorations, gifts for the needy) as well as the midnight Eucharist and carols of Church custom. So with weddings and funerals, baptisms and confirmations—each parish has its own pattern of preparing for these times, its own furnishings to use.

Ideas from sources outside the parish about observing Christian celebrations can be helpful to the priest and the worship committee as they develop their own patterns. Books with suggestions are available and diocesan liturgical commissions are a good resource.[23] Ultimately, liturgy grows out of the group that worships. How to decorate, what to wear, how to set up for each occasion are determined by local circumstances and plans for these occasions within the framework of the Prayer Book are parochial.

Plans are necessary, however, because parish altar workers have to have directions to follow in preparing the worship place. Especially carefully detailed planning is required for occasions involving many people, for example Confirmation, the Dedication of a Church or the Easter Vigil. Once again the need for a parish manual and a working worship committee is evident. A general manual would be even less helpful parish to parish, diocese to diocese, for special occasions than it would be for regular times of the Church. This was not always so, but it is today, and while it may have been simpler and surer to be an altar worker then, it is more interesting and more challenging now.

The Challenge

God is forever calling his children to worship him, to present their lives at the altar imperfect as they may be, to offer him the gifts he has given them. This offering is a means of Grace. The worship of a parish family is this kind of offering. It is a gift expressing the parish life as it is at any given time and it too is a means of Grace.

The Church has inherited certain ways of performing the central action of the Eucharist and the other sacraments, ways that spoke for other times and other places. The challenge to the Church today, to every parish of the Church, is to explore new ways of carrying out the familiar actions, new ways that speak for this time and each place.

The challenge to every altar guild is to prepare for itself with the help of its priest a set of guidelines which allows for this kind of exploration and at the same time covers the essential information altar guilds need in order to understand and carry out their ministry in their separate places. *The Altar Guild Book* has purposely refrained from prescribing exact procedures for altar guilds in favor of describing various practices and furnishings of the Church of yesterday and today. The book is not intended to direct altar guilds in their work, only to give them background for preparing their own guidelines.

Many parishes already have such guidelines. In some instances the priest has prepared them, in some the altar guild itself, in some the two together. These guidelines are written for the present time, anticipating inevitable change. Guidelines written in this way free altar guild workers to prepare their places of worship without rigidity and to offer their gifts and themselves freely in their ministry.

Appendix

I

National, Provincial and Diocesan Altar Guild Organization

Beyond their basic purpose of serving as resource centers for parish altar guilds, each larger altar guild organization has its own special charge. The National Association of Diocesan Altar Guilds is responsible to the Presiding Bishop and carries on its activities through an executive board of seven. It attends to the ecclesiastical needs of the national church—the Presiding Bishop, altars like that at church headquarters in New York, and extra-diocesan branches of the Church like the Armed Forces. It is supported by contributions from the dioceses and by voluntary contributions. Every third year at the time and place of General Convention, the board meets for a week with all the diocesan altar guild directresses for an informative program, a corporate communion, an exhibition of ecclesiastical art from the dioceses, a general business meeting and the election of officers. (The names of current NADAG officers are listed in the *Episcopal Church Annual*, normally found in every parish church office.)

In some provinces, diocesan altar guild directresses have organized loosely to further their basic purpose of relaying information. Leadership rotates among the members. Meetings and conferences are for fellowship, worship and new ideas.

A diocesan altar guild is responsible to the bishop whom it serves. The directress and other officers are normally appointed or at least approved by him, and their activities beyond the ones common to all these larger organizations are determined by the bishop's wishes. Some are involved in many aspects of diocesan life, some attend only to the bishop, diocesan events and non-parochial diocesan altars. Some are comprised of just an executive board, others include parish altar guild directresses as well; still others include all parish altar guild members in the diocese. Most diocesan altar guilds meet at least once a year for a corporate communion, instructive program and annual reports, and most receive support for their projects through voluntary contributions. (Names of DAG presidents are also listed in the *Episcopal Church Annual* under "Altar Guilds.")

II

Equipment for a Useful Sacristy

A useful housekeeping sacristy has a sink big enough for cleaning and laundry tasks and also for working with the largest flower containers. It also has a piscina (a sink that drains directly into the ground for rinsing vessels and linens that have been used in the Eucharist). If there is no piscina, a plastic bowl can be substituted for this rinsing, the rinse water then being emptied on the ground. If there is only a piscina, it is used just for vessels and linens, general sink work being done in another place. If there is no plumbing, water can be carried in for the rinsing.

The useful sacristy also has counter space or a table top large enough for the guild's necessary workspace, including laying out vestments, if that is done (see vestment preparation section), and drying small laundered linens, if that is done (see linen care section). It has mops, broom, vacuum cleaner, dustcloths and similar house-keeping helpers; soaps, polishes and other cleaning substances; towels and at least two dishpans—one for linens and vessels (preferably plastic to protect them), the other for general use. It has a comprehensive guide for spot removal and an assortment of basic stain removal aids. It has an ironing board and iron for touchup pressing, even if regular ironing is done elsewhere; a church calendar, a clock, a wastebasket and a full-length mirror; plain and padded hangers, tissue paper for padding and wrapping, and both cloth and plastic garment storage bags of different sizes; materials for any sewing emergency, including threads matching all the vestments in use, safety pins, a tape measure and a yardstick; a carton of matches, a box of tissues, and first aid supplies including aspirin, cough drops and smelling salts; handy tools like scissors, tongs, screw driver and paring knives; and various mechanics, tools, and containers for flower arranging—unless these are more conveniently kept in a separate place. The equivalent of desk space is desirable, not only for writing but for storing writing materials, altar guild instructions and books, the parish service register, cards and a street map for altar flower delivery to homes and hospitals. A bulletin board for notices is important.

In addition to being well equipped for housekeeping, a useful working sacristy provides storage spaces for all the items used in the worship life of the parish from chalice and paten and bread and wine to the Christmas crèche, the Advent wreath and wedding kneelers. A church uses an incredible amount of paraphernalia in its worship life. It is up to the sacristy housekeepers to devise a way to store it all carefully and yet have it readily available.

<h1 style="text-align:center">III</h1>

The Flower Garden and the Altar

Reprinted with permission of the authors Jeanne Edwards and Sandra Hynson. Copyright National Cathedral Association—"Cathedral Age" Spring 1981.

Spiraling prices over recent years have caused all of us to make significant changes in our working and buying habits. We have had to devise more efficient ways to accomplish a task and to use acceptable substitutes. As volunteers on our church altar guilds we have been doing our share so that we may continue to enhance the worship of God through our ministry of altar adornment.

There is one problem we all share. That is the ever increasing strain on our budgets for items which cannot be changed. While rectors and vestries wrestle with increasing fuel costs, higher salaries and staggering maintenance charges we must continue to buy candles, wine and bread, and replace worn linens and vestments. In respect to altar flowers we are faced with two unique problems which, if attacked with determination and a good deal of ingenuity, can be solved. Indeed the result may be increased effectiveness, a new dimension of spiritual life and greater personal satisfaction.

The first problem revolves around the flowers themselves. Their prices are up because of higher labor costs, packing, shipping and storage expenses. These inflated prices fluctuate dramatically from high to intolerable. Many greenhouses have closed down because of heating costs. Therefore we are more dependent on field-grown flowers which are subject to the capriciousness of the weather.

The second dilemma we face is memorial and/or thanksgiving gifts. A gift of $15 to $25 was sufficient several years ago to purchase flowers to create a fine arrangement; today it is not enough. The gift that remains in that range has an ever decreasing purchasing power as the flowers themselves continue to go up in price.

There are a number of concrete ways to cut costs but the success of these measures depends on educating the congregation to new ideas. If the clergy and altar guild work together and present these budget-saving plans to the parishioners, most will understand and accept them.

Many churches have memorial flowers for Sundays during the year. Often the donors have a standing order with a florist for certain flowers on "their" Sunday. This may result in very lavish flowers one week, a small display for another or some Sundays with no donors. Therefore, a modification of this practice is needed. Ask each donor to contribute money to a revolving altar flower fund. These gifts are collected for the year and placed in a savings account. In addition to earned interest, which will help defray the costs of a few festival extras, more of the congregation can be involved. Additional contributions smaller than a gift to decorate the altar for a Sunday may be made to the fund. All who have designated Sundays retain them and altar guild arrangers can maintain the donor's wishes for choice of flowers and color.

Arrangements of evergreen during the semi-penitential season of Advent, and bare altars during Lent, not only speak symbolically but are great saving. It might be suggested that donors who make their gifts for Sundays during these seasons move their gifts to Christmas or Easter. It can still be stated in Sunday leaflets that prayers are offered for the loved one on his or her special date, but that the flowers are deferred until Christmas or Easter.

In Washington Cathedral wedding flowers remain on the altar as the bride's gift for the Sunday service. With a number of weddings a year this lovely practice provides exquisite flowers for the Sunday congregations to enjoy.

The final and most important point is that the altar guild should order the flowers and arrange them. This system eliminates the florists' labor costs from the budget.

During the winter months one can stretch the budget by buying fewer flowers and arranging them with local evergreens. Become innovative. Use sleeping material such as spirea thunbergii, euonymus alatis, bare branches, azalea, privet, ilex, evergreens of all kinds and/or bare bamboo "pipes." It is surprising how effective an altar arrangement can be when only five gladioli for each container are combined with magnolia leaves which have been washed and burnished with a soft cloth. One might try magnolia soulangeana, eucalyptus and white chrysanthemums. Consider using house plants such as sanseveria arranged with asparagus fern and a few roses.

Learn to force material into bloom—forsythia, quince, plum, willow and others. As soon as Christmas is over begin to "force" a bit from the outdoors. It will do wonders for your arrangements. Plan ahead and keep records. Almost everything takes two to four weeks to force into bloom. Bring your branches indoors, place them in warm water in a sunny window with morning sun if possible. Keep them in the same place and container. They don't like to be disturbed. If forced branches emerge early, wrap in brown paper and store in a very cool place with the stems in water. The forced blossoms will hold for a few days.

Before buying flowers, make a little sketch so that you will have a general idea of the design you would like to try. Go to the florist personally to select the flowers. Once there be flexible; the flowers you had planned on using may not be available. Ask the florist to let you look over his stock and choose the freshest material with crisp leaves. Look for unusual greens which might be substituted for flowers. These could be held over to the following week for use in another way. Most florists are eager to share their knowledge and expertise . . .

One should keep in mind that altar or memorial flowers need not be commercially grown. Given a choice, what could be lovelier than Queen Anne's lace instead of carnations or nandina in lieu of Baker fern? The very act of growing plants or gathering beautiful wild material for the altar is a gift of love. Make good use of those months when God splashes our countrysides and gardens with forsythia and jonquils, zinnias and marigolds, chrysanthemums and berries. With the approval of the congregation you will have a bountiful supply of plant material available.

Securing such materials is an interesting challenge. As you drive to the market keep your eyes open. When you spot a likely bush, tree or patch of grass and weeds make a mental note. Be nosey. If you hear the sound of trees being pruned go and see what is available for your greens. Learn to knock on doors in the neighborhood. Most people are happy to share and will prune shrubbery with you in mind if you let them know. When you are in someone's garden, open your eyes and look around. Keep a list of who has what material . . . People love to share their treasures. However, no one welcomes a heavy-handed pruner. It is better to select a few blossoms from several locations. Never cut more flowers than will be needed in your design. It is surprising how helpful and cooperative city and county officials can be if you ask for a branch or two once in a while. Be sure to request permission to cut either on public domain or in a private field. No trespassing signs mean just that, but most landowners will willingly permit wildflowers to be cut for a church altar . . . Check your local endangered list and never deplete a stand of wild material so that it cannot reseed itself. Encourage the church grounds committee to plant a cutting garden and shrubs with an eye toward pruning for use in your altar arrangements.

Now that you have located desired material the next step is to gather it. Two items are necessary, a trusted cutting tool and plenty of water. Just as the artist must have supple, clean brushes, the chef his sharp steel knives, so the flower arranger must invest in a fine pair of scissors or clippers. Take them with you when you go collecting. Always wipe them dry after use. Don't cut wire with them and don't lend them. Buy them and protect them. The other important item to have with you on such an expedition is water, especially during the hot summer months. Water with a chemical additive, such as vinegar or Floralife, is even better. Wilted flowers can be revived after a hot car ride but they will never again attain the freshness and beauty of the moment of cutting. Try to do your gathering early in the day before the sun warms the flowers and the leaves lose sustaining moisture. Clip each stem under water and place it in your transporting water containers. By using folded or crumpled newspaper in the bucket you can help support the stems and keep the water from spilling in the car.

Now you are ready to bring the flowers and greens home for final conditioning overnight. Since bacteria and air clogging the stems are the two major causes of flower loss, they must be prevented. Spotlessly clean holding containers and stems stripped of leaves below the water line will correct most bacteria problems.

Preventing air in the stem which robs the flowers of moisture is almost a science in itself. Practice using the four basic methods— water, vinegar, fire and chemical. Many plants respond to different methods at different seasons. For example, in the spring maple should have its bark stripped, be cut under water, conditioned in alcohol (whiskey/vodka type) for one minute and finally plunged into deep water. However, in the fall when the maple is older and seasoned it is only necessary to use the vinegar method (one part vinegar to three or four parts water). There is no complete list covering all seasons and conditions in regard to preservation of flower material. If we can suggest only one rule it is the basic water method.

Prevent air from entering the stem by cutting each stem under water. This method is fail safe for most of the material you gather. With certain wild and garden flowers the boiling water method will immediately revive a drooping head. Wrap the bouquet in newspaper to prevent steam damage, but leave the stems exposed. Dip the stem ends into about an inch of boiling water for, one minute for soft stems; three minutes for a fibrous outside but soft inside stems; five minutes for woody branches. Then plunge into cool, deep water to condition overnight. (For additional information on conditioning, see *Homage Through Flowers* by Sandra S. Hynson and the Washington Cathedral Altar Guild.)

We have three suggestions for transporting your conditioned materials to the church sacristy. The best method is to take your flowers in a bucket of water. Wrap the forced material in thin plastic dry cleaner bags and secure the top and bottom with staples to protect the delicate buds. If material is too tall to stand up in the car, and particularly if it is a very hot day, create a "refrigerator." Line one long side of a large plastic bag with wet newspapers. Add a few ice cubes under the paper. Lay the flowers on the cool wet newspapers. Gather the open end of the bag in your hands and blow air into the bag. Quickly secure the opening to trap the air inside. The flowers can now be transported in air conditioned comfort.

After you arrive at the church pause a moment before beginning your arrangements, say a prayer, reflect on the beauty of God's materials which you are about to arrange for his holy table. Then begin. Allow enough time to enjoy the arranging. It can be a chore or it can be exciting, fulfilling, a very personal, experience. Into your hands has come an opportunity to learn and grow. It could add a new dimension to your spiritual life. Don't let it pass by.

IV

Suggestions for Removal of Common Stains

The common stains that altar guilds encounter are wine, lipstick, candlewax, soot, scorch, mildew, blood and rust. The sooner any stain is treated after spotting, the easier its removal. Having a stain removal chart included in the sacristy handbook or posted where altar workers can easily refer to it is a good idea. It is also wise to keep supplies of the common products used in stain removal with the rest of the cleaning equipment in the sacristy. Alcohol, ammonia, club soda, three percent peroxide, table salt and turpentine are all useful home remedies for spots, gentler than many commercial spot removal agents. Every housekeeper has pet ways for removing specific stains. The following all work, but undoubtedly there are others that work equally well.

Blood

Sponge the stain if possible with a small piece of white cloth wet with the saliva of the person whose blood it is. Otherwise soak a fresh blood spot in several changes of cold water and then wash with white soap. Soak a set blood spot in a half and half solution of three percent peroxide and ammonia, and then wash.

Candlewax

On wood or stone: Soften the wax with a hair dryer, wipe off with a paper towel, and rinse the wood or stone with a solution of vinegar and water. Scraping will scratch.

On unlacquered brass and other metals: Pour boiling water over the article or immerse the article in it and swirl. Wipe the article immediately with a paper towel. Repeat if necessary. Use a separate bowl so waxy water will not clog the sink drain.

On lacquered brass and other metal: Use the hair dryer method, but do not rinse with vinegar.

On linen: Remove excess wax by scraping the article gently with a dull implement like the back of a knife. Pour a small amount of turpentine onto the spot, then wash with soap and water. The odor will dissipate and the residual stain should disappear. Or, place the spot in a sandwich of white blotters or brown paper (not paper towels) and iron it with a moderately hot iron. The wax will be absorbed into the blotters. Repeat with fresh blotters if necessary. Sponge any residual stain with alcohol or salt and lemon juice or detergent or a commercial degreaser and wash.

On cloth other than linen: The blotting paper and iron method works on many materials, but not all. Proceed with care, and if in doubt, consult a dry-cleaner.

On carpets: Use the blotting paper and iron method and sponge any residual stain with cleaning fluid.

Lipstick

Apply liquid detergent directly to the spot and rub gently until the stain disappears. Then rinse. Repeat if necessary. Three percent peroxide and ammonia, mixed half and half, can be used on white materials and cleaning fluid on non-washables.

Mildew

Light mildew can usually be removed by laundering with soap and water, rinsing well and drying in the sun. If this method does not work, soak washables in three percent peroxide before washing. Non-washables have to be dry-cleaned. Heavy mildew may be impossible to remove.

Rust

Cover stain with cream of tartar and immerse it in hot water for five minutes, then wash. Or moisten the stain, sprinkle it with salt, wet it thoroughly with lemon juice, and dry it in the sun. Or wet the stain, apply lemon juice and hold it over boiling water so the steam penetrates.

Scorch

For non-washables, soak a press cloth with peroxide, lay it over the stain and iron with a warm iron. If the material is colorfast, sponge the stain with peroxide and rinse.

Soot, Ashes, Smoke

For washables, rub liquid detergent into the stain and rinse. Repeat if necessary. Sponge non-washables with cleaning fluid until the stain goes. If a trace remains, rub it with synthetic detergent and rinse.

Wine

For washables, sprinkle the stain with salt and pour boiling water through it or sprinkle it with salt, immerse it in cold water and rub the stain out. Non-washables with wine stains should go to a dry cleaner.

V

Church Needlework

The following books about ecclesiastical stitchery (and several others) are available from the National Association of Diocesan Altar Guilds Lending Library at the Convent of the Holy Nativity, 101 East

Division Street, Fond du Lac, Wisconsin 54935. Most good public libraries contain a similar assortment.

Patricia Agnew, *Needlepoint for Churches*. Provides well-illustrated stichery, good color plates and excellent advice throughout.

Patricia Beese, *Embroidery for the Church*. Also excellent. Very contemporary in design and material. She uses machine as well as macrame embroidery.

Beryl Dean, *Church Needlework*.
     Ecclesiastical Embroidery.
     Embroidery for Religion and Ceremonial.
     Ideas for Church Embroidery.
The foremost authority in the field.

Joan Edwards, *Church Kneelers*. A small concise book for beginners. Her designs are contemporary, her instructions meticulous. Can be used as a single reference.

Marion P. Ireland, *Textile Art in the Church*. Excellent reference for all church needle arts.

Mary Olsen, *For the Greater Glory*. Probably the best, all-inclusive contemporary book on needlepoint in the church.

Louise Raynor and Carolyn Kerr, *Church Kneelers*. A small basic book with simple and easy designs.

Lilla Weston, *Vestments and How to Make Them*. Not contemporary but helpful.

VI

Vesting Prayers

In the past in some parishes of the Episcopal Church, priests have said the following old prayers while donning the traditional Eucharistic vestments. Some priests still follow the practice.

The Amice

Place, O Lord, the helmet of salvation upon my head, to repel the assaults of the devil.

The Alb

Cleanse me, O Lord, and purify my heart, that washed in the Blood of the Lamb, I may attain everlasting joy.

The Girdle

Gird me, O Lord, with the girdle of purity, and quench in me the fire of concupiscence, that the grace of temperance and chastity may abide in me.

The Maniple

*Grant me, O Lord, to bear the light burden of grief and sorrow,
that I may with gladness receive the reward of my labor.*

The Stole

*Give me again, O Lord, the robe of immortality which I lost by
the sin of my first parents, and although I am unworthy to
come unto thy Holy Sacrament, grant that I may attain everlasting felicity.*

The Chasuble

*O Lord, who has said "my yoke is easy and my burden is
light," grant that I may so bear it as to attain thy grace.*

The Dalmatic or Tunicle

*The Lord clothe me with the garment of salvation and cover
me with the robe of righteousness.*

Notes

1. Title III, Canon 20. Sec. 1 (a), *Constitutions and Canons for the
Government of the Protestant Episcopal Church in the United States of
America, Adopted in General Convention 1789-1973* (New York: Seabury
Press, 1974), p. 83: "The control of the worship and the spiritual jurisdiction
of the Parish are vested in the Rector, subject to the Rubrics of the Book of
Common Prayer, the Canons of the Church, and the godly counsel of the
Bishop. All other Ministers of the Parish, by whatever name they may be
designated, are to be regarded as under the authority of the Rector."

2. John Baillie, *Diary of Private Prayer* (Chas. Scribner and Sons, New
York, 1949), p. 63.

3. Percy Dearmer, *The Parson's Handbook* (Milwaukee: The Young
Churchman Co., 1903), pp. 172, 173.

4. Marion J. Hatchett, *Sanctifying Life, Time and Space* (New York:
Seabury Press, 1976), ch. VIII passim, especially pp. 145, 151-159.

5. W. Appleton Lawrence, *Parsons, Vestries and Parishes* (Greenwich:
Seabury Press, 1961), p. 183.

6. Lawrence, p. 184.

7. Dearmer, p. 97; Hatchett, p. 158.

8. An excellent book about flowers for the altar is *Homage Through
Flowers* by Sandra Hynson (Head of the Washington Cathedral Altar Guild),
see list of sources. Mrs. Hynson together with Jeanne Edwards, has also
written a practical guide to collecting and using field flowers which is included
in this book as Appendix III.

9. Massey Shepherd, *At All Times and In All Places* (New York: Seabury Press, 1965), and Hatchett, op. cit., both passim. For further information about the subject of this chapter, consult also the following books listed in the sources: Edwards, *How It All Began*; Evans, *Prayer Book Renewal*; Hovda, *Strong, Loving and Wise*; Kay, *It Is Your Own Ministry*; Ladd, *Prayer Book Interleaves*; Micks, *The Future Present*; Porter, *Keeping the Church Year*; Pregnall, *Laity and Liturgy*; Price and Weil, *Liturgy for Living*.

10. Hatchett, p. 9.

11. Recipes for Pita (mid-east, Syrian) bread are in many standard cookbooks. The one in *Julia Child and Company* (New York: Alfred A. Knopf, Inc., 1978) is particularly easy to follow and gives good results. *The Book of Bread*, Phillis Nobel, editor, (New York: Seabury Press, 1975) offers many bread recipes, all suitable for the Eucharist.

12. William Temple, *The Hope of a New World* (New York: Macmillan, 1941), pp. 69-71, passim.

13. Hatchett, *A Manual of Ceremonial for the New Prayer Book* (Sewanee: The School of Theology, University of the South, 1977), p. 10.

14. The Cathedral of St. John in the Wilderness, Denver, Colorado, has a beautiful frontal made of old lace pieces.

15. *Caring for Your Linens* (Rye, New York: C. M. Almy and Son); *The Care of Linen* (Davenport, Iowa: Mary Moore); Alma Chestnut Moore, *How to Clean Everything* (New York: Simon and Schuster, 1977), all passim.

16. Charles P. Price and Louis Weil, *Liturgy for Living* (New York: Seabury Press, 1979), p. 90.

17. For example the following books (which are the principal sources of information for this chapter): Cyril E. Pocknee, *Liturgical Vesture, Its Origins and Development* (London; A. R. Mowbray & Son, 1960); J. G. Davies, editor, *The Westminster Dictionary of Worship* (Philadelphia: The Westminster Press, 1972); Christie C. Mayer-Thurman, *Raiment for the Lord's Service, A Thousand Years of Western Vestments* (Chicago: The Art Institute, 1975); and Dom Gregory Dix, *The Shape of the Liturgy* (London: Dacre Press, 1964) ch. 12.

18. Hatchett, *Sanctifying Life, Time, and Space*, p. 145.

19. Cyril E. Pocknee, *Liturgical Vesture* (London: A. R. Mowbray & Co., 1960), p. 48.

20. Kenneth Walter Cameron, editor, *The Church of England in Pre-Revolutionary Connecticut* (Hartford: Transcendental Books, 1976), Letter from Chas. Inglis to Samuel Seabury, p. 235.

21. Dearmer, pp. 146-148.

22. The Merrimac River Valley Textile Museum, North Andover, Massachusetts, is one such museum.

23. Among these books of suggestions are H. Boone Porter, Jr., *Keeping the Church Year* (New York: Seabury Press, 1977) and Marion J. Hatchett, *A Manual of Ceremonial for the New Prayer Book* (Sewanee: The School of Theology, University of the South, 1977).

Bibliography

Books

The Book of Common Prayer according to the Use of the Episcopal Church. New York: The Church Hymnal Corporation and the Seabury Press, 1977.

Booty, John E. *The Church in History.* New York: The Seabury Press, 1979.

Buckland, Patricia B. *Advent to Pentecost, A History of the Christian Year.* Wilton, CT: Morehouse-Barlow, Co. Inc., 1977.

Cameron, Kenneth Walter, editor. *The Church of England in Pre-Revolutionary Connecticut.* Hartford: Transcendental Books, 1976.

Davies, J. G., editor. *The Westminster Dictionary of Worship.* Philadelphia: The Westminster Press, 1972.

Dearmer, The Rev. Percy. *The Parson's Handbook.* Milwaukee: The Young Churchman Co., 1903.

Dix, Gregory. *The Shape of the Liturgy* (passim). London: Dacre Press. Adam and Charles Black, 1964.

Edwards, O. C. *How It All Began.* New York: The Seabury Press, 1973.

Evans, H. Barry, editor. *Prayer Book Renewal.* New York: The Seabury Press, 1978.

Hatchett, Marion J. *Commentary on the American Prayer Book,* "The Holy Eucharist," pp. 289-422. New York: The Seabury Press, 1981.

_____ *A Manual for Ceremonial for the New Prayer Book.* Sewanee: The School of Theology, University of the South, 1977.

_____ *Sanctifying Life, Time, and Space*: An Introduction to Liturgical Study. New York: The Seabury Press, 1976.

Hovda, Robert. *Strong, Loving and Wise.* Washington, D.C.: The Liturgical Conference.

Hynson, Sandra S. *Homage Through Flowers,* A Handbook. Glen Burnie, MD: French/Bray Printing Co., 1978.

Kay, Melissa, editor. *It Is Your Own Ministry.* Washington, D.C.: The Liturgical Conference.

Ladd, William Palmer. *Prayer Book Interleaves.* New York: Oxford University Press, 1943.

Lawrence, W. Appleton. *Parsons, Vestries and Parishes, A Manual,* Chapter 15. Greenwich, CT: Seabury Press, 1961.

Mayer-Thurman, Christie C. *Raiment for the Lord's Service: A Thousand Years of Western Vestments.* Chicago: The Art Institute, 1975.

Micks, Marianne H. *The Future Present.* New York: The Seabury Press, 1977.

Pocknee, Cyril E. *Liturgical Vesture Its Origin and Development.* (Alcuin Club Tracts XXX). London: A. R. Mowbray & Co., 1960.

Porter, H. Boone, Jr. *Keeping the Church Year.* New York: The Seabury Press, 1977.

Pregnall, William S. *Laity and Liturgy, A Handbook for Parish Worship.* New York: The Seabury Press, 1975.

Price, Charles P. *Introducing the Proposed Book.* New York: The Church Hymnal Corporation, 1976.

_____ and Weil, Louis. *Liturgy for Living.* New York: The Seabury Press, 1979.

Rodenmayer, Robert N. *Thanks Be To God.* New York: Harper and Brothers, 1960.

Shepherd, Massey Hamilton, Jr. *At All Times and In All Places.* New York: The Seabury Press, 1965.

_____, editor. *The Liturgical Renewal of the Church.* New York: Oxford University Press, 1960.

_____ *The Reform of Liturgical Worship.* New York: Oxford University Press, Inc. 1961.

The Standing Liturgical Commission of the Protestant Episcopal Church in the United States of America. *Prayer Book Studies IV, The Eucharistic Liturgy.* New York: The Church Pension Fund, 1953.

Manuals

The Altar Guild Manual of the Diocese of Dallas. Dallas: The Diocese of Dallas, 1977.

The Altar Guild Manual of the Diocese of Minnesota. Minneapolis: The Diocese of Minnesota, 1979.

The Altar Guild Manual: Episcopal Diocese of Oklahoma. Oklahoma City: The Diocese of Oklahoma, 1976.

Diggs, Dorothy C. *A Working Manual for Altar Guilds.* New York: Morehouse-Barlow, Co. Inc., 1973.

McClinton, Katherine Morrison and Squier, Isabel Wright. *Good Housekeeping in the Church.* New York: Morehouse-Gorham Co., 1951.

Perry, Edith Weir. *An Altar Guild Manual.* New York: Morehouse-Barlow, Co., 1963.

Smart, The Rev. Henry. *The Altar: Its Ornaments and Its Care.* Milwaukee: Morehouse Publishing Co., 1925.

Lectures

Dunn, The Rev. Howard Francis. *A History of Church Vestments.* Address to the Connecticut Diocesan Altar Guild, 1960.

Fenhagen, The Very Rev. James C. *Lay Ministry.* Addresses to the Laymen's Conference, Diocese of Connecticut, 1977.

Gushee, The Very Rev. Stephen. *Loose-Leaf Liturgy, Loose-Leaf Altar Guild Manuals.* Address to the Connecticut Diocesan Altar Guild, 1980.

Koch, The Rev. W. Christian. *The Holy Space.* Addresses to the Province I Altar Guild Conference, 1980.

Lowe, The Rev. William. *Christian Renewal and Living Liturgy.* Addresses to the Province I Altar Guild Conference, 1979.

Porter, The Rev. H. Boone, Jr. *The History of the Christian Altar.* Address to the National Association of Diocesan Altar Guilds, 1979.

Porteus, The Rt. Rev. Morgan. Various informal addresses to the Connecticut Diocesan Altar Guild, 1975-1981.

Spencer, The Rev. Bonnell, OHC. *The Altar Guild Ministry Today.* Address to the National Association of Diocesan Altar Guilds, 1973.

Stuhlman, The Rev. Byron. *The New Prayer Book.* Address to the Deanery Liturgical Commission, Hartford, CT, 1977.